You and Contemporary Poetry

Books by George Abbe

George Abbe

YOU AND CONTEMPORARY POETRY

An aid-to-appreciation

RICHARD • R • SMITH
NOONE HOUSE
PETERBOROUGH • NEW HAMPSHIRE

July, 1965

Acknowledgments

Grateful acknowledgment is tendered for the poems and excerpts from poems quoted herein:

ALLING, KENNETH SLADE: "Dead Wasp," *Kingdom of Diamonds*, Indiana University Press, 1954.

BABCOCK, DONALD: "Two Things," *New Poems by American Poets*, edited by Rolfe Humphries, Ballantine Books, Inc., New York, 1953.

BEAUDOIN, KENNETH: "Pastoral Poem," *Eight American Poets*, Villiers Publications, London, 1952.

BISHOP, ELIZABETH: "The Fish," *Poems, North and South: a Cold Spring*, Houghton Mifflin Co., Boston, 1947.

BISHOP, JOAN: "Profile," *Voices*, Summer, 1954.

BJERKNES, CHRIS: "After Love," *Epos*, Winter, 1953; "April," *First Communion*, Olivant House, Fitzgerald, Ga., 1954.

CUMMINGS, E. E.: "A Man Who had Fallen Among Thieves," *Poems 1923 - 1954*, by permission of Harcourt, Brace and World, Inc., New York; copyright 1926 by Horace Liveright, copyright 1954 by e. e. cummings.

DIMMETTE, CELIA: "The Lamb," *The New York Times*, February 17, 1953.

DRAKE, LEAH BODINE: "Honey from the Lion," *Saturday Review*, December 6, 1947.

EBERHART, RICHARD: "Go to the Shine that's on a Tree," *Collected Poems 1930-1960*, Copyright 1960 by Richard Eberhart; Oxford University Press, Inc., New York.

EBERMAN, WILLIS: "After Illness," *Lyric*, Summer, 1954.

ELIOT, T. S.: "The Wasteland," *Collected Poems, 1909-1935*, Harcourt, Brace and World, Inc. New York, 1936.

ELLIOTT, GEORGE P.: "The Gift," *Eight American Poets*, Villiers Publications, London, 1952; "To a Bird Outside the Window," *Poetry*, January, 1947.

iv

FERLINGHETTI, LAWRENCE: "No. 3," *A Coney Island of the Mind*, New Directions, New York, 1958.

GARDNER, ISABELLA: "Gimboling," *Birthdays from the Ocean*, Houghton Mifflin Co., Boston, 1955.

GARRICK, JED: "Answer in Bright Green," *Flame*, Spring, 1955.

GIBSON, WALKER: "Billiards," "The Thaw," *The Reckless Spenders*, Indiana University Press, 1954.

GINSBERG, ALLEN: "Death to Van Gogh's Ear!" *Kaddish and Other Poems, 1958 - 1960*, City Lights Books, San Francisco, 1961.

GLEASON, G. SCOTT: "A Country-Bred Boy," *Lyric*, Summer, 1954.

HARSHBARGER, PAT: "Don't Make the Angels Cry," *Treasures of Parnassus*, Young Publications, Appalachia, Virginia, 1962.

HAY, JOHN: "Town Meeting," *New Poems by American Poets*, edited by Rolfe Humphries, Ballantine Books, New York, 1953.

HOLMES, LAWRENCE: "Ruth for the Mortal," *Epos*, Summer, 1953.

HOPKINS, GERARD MANLEY: "God's Grandeur," *The Poems of G. M. Hopkins*, Oxford Univ. Press, New York.

JACKINSON, ALEX: "Television," *Epos*, Winter, 1953.

JARRELL, RANDALL: "Death of a Ball Turret Gunner," *Little Friend, Little Friend*, The Dial Press, New York, 1945.

JEFFERS, ROBINSON: "The Deer Lay Down Their Bones," *Hungerfield and Other Poems*, by permission of Random House, Inc.; copyright 1945 by Robinson Jeffers.

KINNELL, GALWAY: "To William Carlos Williams," *What a Kingdom It Was*, Houghton Mifflin Co., Boston, 1960.

LIPTON, LAWRENCE: "Inquest," "Fanfare for a Delayed Exit," "With Einstein's Fiddle," *Rainbow at Midnight*, Golden Quill Press, Francestown, N. H., 1955.

LORRAINE, LILITH: "Calling All Grandchildren," *Flame*, Winter, 1953.

MASTERS, MARCIA: "Childhood," *Voices*, Fall, 1953.

MAYS, JOHN BARRON: "The Surgeon," *Epos*, Winter, 1953.

McGAFFIN, AUDREY: "Inertia," *New Poems by American Poets*, edited by Rolfe Humphries, Ballantine Books, Inc., New York, 1953.

MOONEY, ALFRED: "Love's Season," by permission of the author.

MOORE, MERRILL: "Mrs. Broderick was a very unusual woman," *Clinical Sonnets*, Twayne Publishers, New York, 1949.

PATCHEN, KENNETH: "O Fiery River," *Selected Poems*, New Directions Publishers, New York, 1957.

PENNER, GEORGE: "Prescription for Faint Hearts," *The Contemporary Reader*, January, 1955.

PILLIN, WILLIAM: "Folk Song," *Dance Without Shoes*, Golden Quill Press, Francestown, N. H., 1956.

POUND, EZRA: "Canto XLV," *The Fifth Decad of Cantos*, New Directions, New York, 1937.

ROETHKE, THEODORE: "The Sloth," *New Poems by American Poets*, edited by Rolfe Humphries, Ballantine Books, Inc., 1953.

SCHEVILL, JAMES: "Confidential Data on the Loyalty Investigation of Herbert Ashenfoot," *Private Dooms and Public Destinations: Poems 1945 - 1962*, Alan Swallow, Denver, 1962; "Ralph Waldo Emerson," *Eight American Poets*, Villiers Publications, London, 1952.

SCOTT, WINFIELD TOWNLEY: "The U. S. Sailor and the Japanese Skull," *To Marry Strangers*, Thomas Y. Crowell, New York, 1945.

SHAPIRO, KARL: "Buick," *Poems, 1940 - 1953*, Random House Inc., New York, 1953.

SIMPSON, LOUIS: "The Ash and the Oak," *New Poems by American Poets*, edited by Rolfe Humphries, Ballantine Books Inc., New York, 1953.

STEFANILE, FELIX: "Village on My Back," "The Marionettes," "That Underground Sun," *Eight American Poets*, Villiers, London, 1952.

THOMAS, DYLAN: "If I were tickled by the rub of Love," *The Collected Poems of Dylan Thomas*, New Directions, New York.

TURKAT, JUDAH M.: "Faces Before," *Epos*, Winter, 1953.

WESTON, ADELAIDE: "Feathered in Sun," *Lyric*, Summer, 1954.

WHITMAN, WALT: "When Lilacs last in the Dooryard Bloom'd," *Leaves of Grass*, Doubleday and Co., New York, 1940.

WILBUR, RICHARD: "A Simile for Her Smile," "Death of a Toad," *Ceremony, And Other Poems*, Harcourt, Brace and World, Inc., New York; copyright 1948, 1949, 1950 by Richard Wilbur.

WILLIAMS, JAMES K.: "Bliss can be yours," by permission of the author.

WILLIAMS, WILLIAM CARLOS: "To a Dog Injured in the Street," by permission of New Directions, New York; copyright 1953 by William Carlos Williams.

YEATS, WILLIAM BUTLER: Lines from "Crazy Jane Talks with the Bishop," *Collected Poems*, The Macmillan Co., New York, 1933.

The author also wishes to express his appreciation for brief quotations from the following articles:

CIARDI, JOHN: "An Ulcer, Gentlemen, is an Unwritten Poem," Canadian Business, Montreal, June, 1955. COPELAND, GEORGE: "Debussy, the Man I Knew," *The Atlantic*, January, 1955. JUNG, C. G.: "Psychology, East and West," *Tomorrow*, Vol. 4, No. 1.

Grateful acknowledgment is also made to the editors of *Writer's Digest, Poetry Public, Trace, Coastlines,* and *The Sparrow*, who first published portions of this book in their pages. The author's own poems, "Traffic Quince," "Horizon Thong," "Mowing the Lawn," "The Garage," and "The Book" are from *Collected Poems, 1932 - 1961*, Richard R. Smith Co., Inc., Peterborough, New Hampshire.

Author's Note

A SPECIAL WORD of gratitude is due Lawrence Holmes, Associate Professor of English at Hastings College, Hastings, Nebraska, and founder and editor of *Poetry Public* magazine, for his editorial help and contribution in the preparation of the first chapter, especially that part dealing with the background of modern poetry.

I wish to express my appreciation to Dr. Philmore Wass and his wife, Dorothy, for their enthusiastic help in launching the "poetry-in-the-round" experiments in the schools and writing up the first report of the results, part of which has been incorporated in the final chapter of this book.

I am deeply indebted to Percy McNutt, who gave me the idea in the first place, to William L. Bauhan, my editor and publisher, for his unceasing labor with the manuscript, and lastly to the many poets who have generously permitted me to quote from their work.

G. A.

Contents

The Modern Idiom

WHY ARE SO MANY PEOPLE impatient with modern poetry? Why is it that some of the most intelligent readers today avoid it? Why do so many others respond only to the harmless, the sportive, or the sentimental? Contemporary poetry is too "difficult," it is said, hard to "understand," or too "far out." The trite and the familiar, the sexy and violent continue to attract, because they are easy-to-acquire, but they make little demand upon the total person. Artistic vitality implies not only a unique completeness of self on the part of the artist, but requires an equal fulness of response, an equal application, in the reader — whether his reaction happens to mesh with the individuality of the author, or not. "To have great poets," wrote Harriet Monroe, "there must be great audiences, too."

The best poem, past or present, is resistant; it demands effort, application, to break through to the inviolable identity within. If the modern poem is distinguished by greater "resistance," if it is more "difficult" and complex, is it any more than a valid reflection of the complexity and multiplicity of our own age?

Modern poetry as such is not false, degenerate, or obscure, as some have tried to make out. It is different, because human beings and circumstances have changed. Poets are, by and large, still the same compassionate, sensitive folk they were fifty or one hundred years ago: intuitive, suffering, hopeful; as Paul Engle said, "They are like everyone else, only more so." Their experiences have not changed basically; but their mode and manner of expressing them have. They are digging for clams in the same mud flats humanity knew a thousand years ago, but the tides go out farther now because strange moons pull at our earth, moons of cataclysm. Their motions may be more lean and nervous and intense, the thrust of their hoes more rapacious; but the urgent strength is there, the concern for life and people.

Is the world today too driven to imbibe the poetic? Is it a fact that American art by and large means only entertainment, escape? On all of us, today, the pressures of mere survival are indeed enormous. We find it difficult to bring extra energy to any art that makes demands upon emotion and creativity of thought. Music, painting, and drama are more immediate arts than poetry; no matter how complex, they have a more direct sensory appeal, and in their modern forms they have overtaken poetry in popular favor. Poetry requires more effort, today, especially; it calls upon *all* our powers; it is drama and music and painting, all compounded and compressed. It may be relished at every level; and for this reason it can be the most rewarding of the arts — but the richer the reward is to be, the greater must be the investment.

One reason, then, that the modern poet and his work are misunderstood is that too many of us fail to make the effort to understand. Submit ourselves to the first steps of analysis and honest appraisal, and we'll find many new excitements unfolding. To learn to play the piano, we had, as children, to do finger exercises many tedious hours. If we undertake even a fraction of such training in the field of poetry, our enrichment will be immeasurable.

Is the misunderstanding all on one side? No. There are valid objections to modern poetry — many readers have tried to appreciate it only to find themselves bewildered, bored, or repelled. This lack of communication is the fault, not of the best contemporary poets, but of coterie poets who write to scratch each other's backs, of extremists whose work is unintelligible, of those who sacrifice idea and content in their search for uniqueness of expression. In one form or another the coteries, the distortions and perversions of poetry-as-art, have persisted throughout the history of literature. But legitimate poetry, the best of it, has always required concentration on the part of the reader, particularly when it is fresh and individual.

To understand the finest in the art demands audience discipline — a practice, an application, a degree of study and training. Only gradually does the unfamiliar and disturbing become assimilated into a culture. It was a long time before Emily Dickinson came to be really enjoyed and understood.

Over and beyond this, there are the practices concerning poetry handed down from a past when the art of poetry was closer to other forms.

Didactic poetry — the lesson poem — was long used to prop up the frail, attenuated frame of a sermon, causing people to associate poetry with sermonizing; and so we have the moral poem, often much too pointed and preachy. Obvious and oversimple verse was used to expound a cause — Women's Rights or Abolition — and so it appeared on the

3

editorial page, and people came in time to expect from poetry the attitudes and emotions of the editorial.

Or poetry was written in conjunction with very regularly cadenced music of the popular sort, and so people began to associate it always with the mechanics of conventional beat and melody.

In the age of the Romantics, it was fashionable to cry out, with Shelley: "I fall upon the thorns of life; I bleed." Much of our popular magazine and women's club poetry continues to voice such views. What was new and exciting in Shelley's time, has — through 150 years of imitation and repetition — become worn, trite, and sentimental in our own. In content such "popular verse" is sticky, didactic, flowery, conventional in thought. It editorializes and attitudinizes, and it perpetuates styles and forms that have little relevance for today. Its ideas are second-third-fourth-hand, watered down, and "ready to serve."

Legitimate poetry, like all good art, is original, sometimes even shockingly so. It must derive its originality through direct personal experience, which can never be *exactly* like anyone else's. One of the prime functions of all art is to give us the familiar in unfamiliar ways, or the unfamiliar in ways that can reach us. As such, good poetry is more *subjective,* and, like what is good in the other arts, it is more genuine and more certain to last.

But apart from the popular versifiers, what of the serious poets of today who write in a "traditional" vein? Again, much of our current "traditional" poetry is enjoyed at a purely sensuous, even superficial, level; it tends to be too "easy." Can a modern imitation of a style that was fresh in 1850 last?

For example, the sonnet as a form was fresh and vigorous in earlier centuries; today it is difficult to make it succeed. (One well-known contemporary editor will not accept a

4

sonnet for his magazine.) Now and then a modern writer does inject new, authentic force into the sonnet, but usually the traditional in form fails today, because it tends to drag down the content with it, to make the inward tone, attitude, spirit as outmoded as the exterior.

If there is an outstanding exception, then perhaps it is Robert Frost. Writing largely in traditional forms, Frost, however, had a highly individual stamp, and his genius lay in an ability to convey universal *ideas* and feelings that have found a receptive readership today. But where will the reader of the twenty-first century place Frost? Is his popularity in this generation due to a nostalgia — a recognition that Frost was attempting to bring to our age values that we hanker for, but in truth no longer possess? Or will the reader of the future look to some of the younger writers, the modern poets, as giving more valid expression to the values, the conditions, the spirit of our times?

We have alluded to some of the characteristics of modern poetry, but what, exactly, do we mean by "modern"? First, modern poetry speaks in the idiom of today as against the idiom of the past; it expresses our modern society, the tone and temper of the hour. Next, it tends to move *away from the obvious,* to create its effects *more indirectly* than did the poetry of preceding generations. (Later on we will examine this particular point more closely.) The poet of the present also seeks original form and style; the arts of all the ages have found their greatest power in such adjustment.

In image and diction, in rhythm and sound, in form and in idea, typically modern poetry is at once distinguishable from the best, as well as from the worst, examples of traditional poetry. It is true that an archaeologist can examine an ancient potsherd and tell when it was made, within a margin of error of fifty years, and that a bright English major can

5

"place" a poem he has never read before within a decade or two of its date of composition through consideration of diction and form. It is likewise true that there has been a greater advance in innovation, though not necessarily in artistry, between, say, 1910 and 1960, than between 1610 and 1910. In other words, three-hundred years or more of poetic evolution have been equalled by half a century of evolution so rapid as to be better described by the word "revolution."

Let us look for a moment at some of the men who shaped modern poetry.

Two nineteenth-century poets, an American and an Englishman, anticipated in very different ways the great twentieth-century revolution in poetry. Walt Whitman, representative of the divine average, great poet of empathy and the mystical oneness of all living things and all mankind — in his own words a person "naive, masculine, affectionate, contemplative, sensual, imperious" — was, as his poetry shows, a self-dramatizing and sometimes shocking sensualist combined with something between a Quaker and a transcendentalist. Whitman abandoned traditional prosody, to the dismay of most of his contemporaries. He wrote a long-lined, Biblical, oratorical free verse, predominantly trochaic and dactylic, employing much alliteration, assonance, and internal rhyme, producing verse which at its most exalted is pure, unpatterned lyricism: "Ever-returning spring, trinity sure to me you bring, / Lilac blooming perennial and drooping star in the west, / And thought of him I love."

Gerard Manley Hopkins, English Jesuit priest and poet, once wrote: " . . . I always knew in my heart Walt Whitman's mind to be more like my own than any other man's living. As he is a very great scoundrel, this is not a very pleasant confession." As concentrated and knottily wrought as Whitman's is expansive, Hopkins' verse, with its "sprung rhythm" and startling aural innovations, is usually crowded within traditional rhyme patterns, as the sonnet. But he is *most* modern in his boldly and passionately original imagery; and his use of assonance, alliteration, and internal rhyme is far more startling than Whitman's, e.g.: "Didst fettle for the great grey drayhorse his bright and battering sandal!"

The Irishman, William Butler Yeats, is in reality two or three poets, at least. In the nineteenth century he was a romantic lyricist, exploiting Celtic tradition and magic: "There midnight's all a glimmer, and noon a purple glow, / And evening full of the linnet's wings." But the twentieth century, with its fearless readiness to grapple ironically with reality, did not find Yeats behindhand; and in the early thirties, he could write: "A woman can be proud and stiff / When on love intent; / But Love has pitched his mansion in / The place of excrement; / For nothing can be sole or whole / That has not been rent."

Private mythology and somewhat esoteric symbolism Yeats turns to far more successful account than one would have dreamed possible; and his later nonromantic lyricism is so distinguished and unforgettable in diction and imagery as to earn him the reputation as one of the greatest twentieth-century poets of the English language.

When one hears the name T. S. Eliot, one thinks of many things — the French Symbolists, the Jacobean dramatists, Donne, Launcelot Andrewes, Fraser's *Golden Bough,* "classicism in literature, royalism in politics, and Anglo-Catholicism in religion" — but most of all one thinks of Eliot's allusiveness, a characteristic typical of much modern poetry. Think of the erudition necessary to comprehend the finale of THE

WASTELAND: "London Bridge is falling down falling down falling down/*Poi s'ascose nel foco che gli affina* . . ./Datta. Dayadhvam. Damyata. Shantih shantih shantih."

Even further than this has Ezra Pound carried allusiveness in some of his CANTOS, where Chinese characters add to the ordinary reader's despair. Thus Pound has contributed to the reputations of more modern poets than has any other one person, Yeats, Frost, and Eliot being only the most famous of these. A great, if somewhat brash, translator (from the Anglo-Saxon, Greek, Latin, Provencal, Chinese), in one sense a traditionalist, in another the most modern of moderns, he looks both backward and forward. A virtuoso of verse forms, a critic with unerring taste and trenchant frankness, and author of one of the most erudite, allusive, and wilfully recondite of poetic works (CANTOS), he can, when it pleases him, speak out eloquently in ringingly clear tones: "Usura slayeth the child in the womb/It stayeth the young man's courting/It hath brought palsey to bed, lyeth/between the young bride and her bridegroom/CONTRA NATURAM."

It would be unfair to charge Eliot, or even Pound, with "cultivated eccentricity," designed to capture attention and provide publicity. The charge would perhaps be slightly justified in the case of e. e. cummings, whose typographical pranks, combined with romantic love sentiment, are almost too well-known to be mentioned here. It is, however, his syntactical acrobatics that constitute his most characteristic and most effective contribution to modern poetic experimentation: "Blow soon to never and never to twice / (blow life to isn't: blow death to was) / — all nothing's only our hugest home; / the most who die, the more we live."

These six poets provide a fair cross section — very incomplete, to be sure — of some of the most significant tendencies in modern poetry: a breaking away from, or a bold modification of, the old rigid verse forms, the exploitation of modern ideas and attitudes to provide the content even of poems more or less traditional in form, allusiveness even to the point of obscurity, greater realism in content and language, innovations in typography and syntax, and greater freedom in subject matter, imagery, and symbolism. To this summary should be added the undeniable generalization that in emotional power and depth, in imaginative daring and breadth, the best of our modern poets are second to none but the five or six all-time world greats.

Movements and countermovements in poetic theory and practice have complicated the picture somewhat, but few will deny the basic contrast, a contrast not dissimilar to the acceleration, within the same period, of scientific knowledge. This is not to stay that poetic artistry has advanced at a rate comparable to that of scientific understanding. It is highly probable that artistry, while it may change in *kind,* does not advance at all in degree of excellence from one millenium to another. In artistry the finest modern poet is scarcely superior to Homer or Sappho. Individual genius is a far more important factor, apparently, in poetry and the other arts, than in science. But the images that poets use must change with advances in natural science and technology. Diction must change with linguistic evolution. Rhythm and sound in poetry must be modified by the rhythm of the times and the sound that the *Zeitgeist* makes.

Yet is is safe to say that in originality, beauty, and power, the best modern poetry differs less from the best traditional poetry than the inferior representatives of each of these classes differ from each other. If representative modern poetry is bold in image and diction, so was Shakespeare. If the wilder of the moderns seem to have abandoned music and form en-

9

tirely, certainly the less gifted poets of the past made fetishes of the more obvious and conventional manifestations of music and form. And if it was the best poets of the past who first surmised that no subject-matter, no image, no diction, no idea under the sun that concerned mankind was outside the province of poetry, it has been the best (as well as the worst) poets of the past fifty years who have probed further, ventured more, and turned up a more fascinating, and in some cases a more appalling, variety of poetic riches than had been turned up in almost the whole previous history of poetry.

Having said this, we must now ask: What, then, will best help the modern reader to appreciate what the modern poet is doing? What will best help him to see that the poet is really expressing what everyone feels, but in new and individual ways which require a little concentration and intimate give-and-take in order to assume a friendly familiarity? What will close the gap between the traditional and the contemporary?

Let us try to approach this greater appreciation by discussing some typically modern poems, seeking to reveal their honesty and strength, as well as their weakness, to show how they carry on the best of our heritage in ways perhaps strange and astonishing, yet eminently worthy; and finally, to discover common denominators, if any, between the traditional poet and the modern.

2

Image and Diction

I SHOULD LIKE to have you consider how modern poetry differs from the traditional poetry in respect to image and diction.

The basic element in poetry is imagery. (Diction, the proper selection of words, we will come back to later.) Without metaphor, without the pictorial, the poem would descend into the limbo of prose. The fundamental difference between the images employed in traditional poetry and modern is that the latter must release the fresh and vividly new. It is not too trite to say that what deadens verse most is triteness.

Many people object to modern verse because they come to it expecting to find the old familiar images, the early-youth patterns of emotion that make them feel soothed and comfortable. But poetry, if it is vital, must advance constantly across imposing frontiers; it must hew cabins of unique and lonely beauty, whose chimney smoke may become romantic only with time.

11

Let us turn for a moment to this stanza from a poem, LOVE'S SEASON, by Alfred L. Mooney:

> O, sweet as painted flowers
> That drew the breath of spring,
> My love to me came smiling
> To urge myself to sing.

A lovely person has been compared to a flower so many times that the effect has withered — unless it be reinforced by unprecedented color and fragrance.

Or take this sonnet, FIRST SNOW, by Lawrence Richard Holmes:*

> Ten trillion fluttering snowflakes from the air
> Lie sparkling on the roofs and boughs and ground,
> Candying the earth for miles around
> With a splendid crystal whiteness, bright and rare.
> This snowfall takes me back a single year,
> When you, my child, were nowhere to be found,
> Before your voice had uttered one small sound,
> Before your eyes had shed their first bright tear.
> The snow fell then, while we awaited you,
> As now it falls to give you new delight,
> And you stare out the window at the white
> Incomparable tingling freshness, too,
> And gasp, ecstatic in your elfin glee,
> At one more gift from Nature's treasury.

The rhymes are hackneyed and sometimes forced: "found," for instance, in line 6, is inaccurate — the child was not lost, but as yet unborn — and "too," in line 12, is padding used

---

* This example — a poem written without tongue in cheek many years ago — has been used here at Mr. Holmes' own suggestion.

to rhyme with "you." The diction, likewise, is trite, especially in lines 4, 13, and 14. "Elfin glee" — elfin this or that — and "gift from Nature's treasury" have been rendered time without number in traditional poetry of the second- and third-rate levels.

Too often, the poet, like the traditional audience, leans upon the recognizable: it is easier, it is less complicated and risky, a sly stroking of the ego's fur.

But now, let us see what a poet can do when he takes a concept and twists it with surprising new power, as tennis champion Pancho Gonzales might employ his wrist in a delicate and explosive volley. Willis Eberman gives us this brief piece, AFTER ILLNESS:

> Keenly aware
> Of light and air,
> The porcelain,
> Pallid, thin
> Cup of the body
> Contains at length
> A glint of strength.

It may well be that the body has been compared to a cup before. Indeed, it would be strange if it had not. But this is a conscious cup, a cup "keenly aware." The body is like "porcelain," a most apt description of sickness-drained flesh. Through this porcelain emanates the glow, faintly, of strength returning *consciously.* That is important: the person really getting well after a severe illness is not only becoming alive, he is now acutely sensitive to all the minutiae of the earth, all that dwells in the ineffable plazas of light and air. That is why the placement of "keenly aware" at the beginning is so apt: it flicks the dial to the right point for all the scenes to follow. Not only is the cup conscious of its own "glint" of returning strength, an emphasis which gives veracity and uniqueness, but there is another trait which makes the image superior to those of the poem quoted earlier. A cup is something to give esthetic pleasure. The body, the life, of the convalescent will now have truer meaning to another. But this is implied, not said. Inference, implication rather than the obvious, and the overstated, help a poem. This short piece is not startling and it is not great; but it contains two important elements in the handling of images: fresh veracity and perception, and understatement.

But, you may say, and quite rightly: "Why is originality of image peculiarly modern? Poets of the past demonstrated the same talent." True. But there is a bluntness in the modern image, an impact quick, hard, uncompromising — often offensive. The original images of the old school were cushioned in full-cadenced lines, complete syntax, well-rounded sentences, long pliant surges that carried the reader effortlessly. Yesterday's poet snared the reader with a swan-boat ride, a butterfly net; today's poet buckles you with an elevator-drop, nicks you with a rifle.

Take, for instance, FEATHERED IN SUN, by Adelaide Weston:

> With a curve of claw
> A cage
> For sleet, and wind
> And rage,
> With a planet
> Glassed in his eye,
> A brightly feathered
> Sky
> Folded wings
> Of the far and wide,

And thirstily
Drank seatide;
Then soared again
To the peak,
And held a star
In his beak.

First of all, the comparison of sky to a feathered bird is unique: the sun, though warm, is seldom thought of as fluffy and downy in consistency. When you reach those words, "a brightly feathered sky," you are hit between the eyes by the idea. It is a bold metaphor, a small-scale revolution. Next to see a curved claw described as a cage for sleet is certainly surprising — harshly, titillatingly so — for who would want to hold onto sleet? And then, the wind — actually, how could a claw hold onto wind? It would slip through. The poet is crazy. But that is why she succeeds: she takes a chance; the verse transcends the merely factual and literal; it challenges, it startles.

Next, "with a planet / glassed in his eye." What an impact is there! Why, yes, the sky, if it were an eagle, or a monster bird, would certainly, quite naturally, look as though it had a planet or a star for an eye. But what aids the effect most is that word "glassed." It is the active form. It is not a "glassy eye," or an "eye of glass." It is "glassed." In the past participle, the performance is felt; someone has done the deed, has acted as agent. Who would bake and cool a planet into the proper-shaped glass for a giant sky-bird's eye? Why, maybe the bird himself. Maybe he melted the sands of the shore in the heat of the sun and made the glass. But why? Because he liked the idea of being odd, grotesque, sardonic; because he wanted to eye the world through something hideously monstrous and artificial, with cynical disdain. Being stuffed with the natural elements of air and light and heat to the point of ennui, he desired something unnatural; he wished to behold the creatures of earth through a huge, distorting lens, for entertainment, to amaze and affright, just as a boy likes to look in crazy mirrors in the amusement park.

The short, irregular lines help the impact, the bizarre titillation, and are a mark of the modern. "A cage" set off by itself adds emphasis to the idea, gives more blunt force; the same is true for "and rage." Make "with a planet / glassed in his eye" one line instead of two: the effect is lost.

And now, see how image drives home its last clinchers, like a sewing machine punching out its final, telling stitches. The sky folds wings "of the far and wide" — a neat and appropriate thought; but then, suddenly, "thirstily drank seatide." Ordinarily, the folding of wings is a calm, satisfied, restful act. How quick-changing, contradictory, excitingly odd is that sudden repairing to the sea to drink up the tide with hasty thirst! But again, how provocative!

"Then soared again / to the peak / and held a star / in his beak." What is the bird doing up there suddenly, holding a star in his beak? And yet, though irrational, the poem has its own inward, intuitive logic. The sky, subject to weather, *is* impulsive; it *is* given to moods. The way the bird acts, then, clinches the emotion in us, the sense of sky as feathery bird — not a scientific account of sky, but the inner essence of it.

Traditional poetry depends more upon the literal and logical connection between ideas, the normal flow of sentence structure, line, thought. It tends to tell all for the reader, fashion the full structure of thought so that little can be supplied by the audience. The poems of former times often were closer to editorial, sermon, or prose in tempo and manner.

16

Today, the poem is streamlined and telescoped, and though the reader's mind must be more active to fill the gaps, that very demand upon him kindles his imagination more and produces a finer flavor of discernment.

The modern image, then, is more abrupt, quick, raw; it leans more toward power; it veers more widely from the literal, nicely connected; it is more implicit, more compressed, more provocative. It assumes an agility in the reader, a willingness to leap rather than walk — which ought certainly to be the characteristic of poetry as compared to prose — and its sincerity or individuality rises from its relevance to the present — and independence of the past.

The modern poet has a proclivity for less romantic, more realistic images — pictures brashly and healthily of the stuff of common day. Observe, for instance, the romantic nature of these lines from A COUNTRY-BRED BOY by G. Scott Gleason:

> He's ruddy, He's slim as a buggy-whip.
> Of field and stream, he's a child.
> He's brown as any bark, swimming-hole eager.
> He's half the woods and wild.

Now, these are the time-honored, delectable attitudes. This is the way the women's magazines would depict a nostalgic childhood. "Ruddy" is a pleasant color. No scraping of doubt, no disquietude, in its connotation. The boy must be slim; he will grow into a tall, dark, sinewy vise of romantic embraces. A buggy-whip has nostalgic connotations of more leisurely and gracious days; indeed, it is a fine symbol of a whole earlier era, glamorous, safe to linger over, because now distant. And "bark" — a good, clean, lovely part of nature — no irritation, no departure from the norm, no argument there. The same with the swimming-hole.

17

G. Scott Gleason has done here a poem that is not poor; in fact, for a romantic poem, it is rather good. I apologize for hacking it apart, but do it for the sake of emphasis: it is still a romantic poem; it selects for amiability. And that is not a trait of the poetry more distinctively modern; instead, it harks back to the age of Longfellow and Tennyson. There was nothing wrong with those poets; they are simply of another day, another view, another constellation of circumstances.

But look, now, at these examples, all by poets who are modern, but not in a dada-bohemian way. First, PROFILE, by Joan Bishop:

> Within his chest
> the mouse of discontent
> scrabbles itself a nest
> of insults kindly meant.
>
> With yesterday's regrets
> it lines a bed of sorrow
> in which to conjure up
> dismay tomorrow.
>
> Only a cat
> of quite substantial art
> could penetrate
> this labyrinthine heart.

Discontent, in the more old-fashioned poetry, might prowl like a satanic lion, or lean like a stricken flower, or act in some such elevated or sugared manner, but it would not be described as a mouse that "scrabbles itself a nest of insults." That is harsh, oblique, a bit gritty, almost offensive. But is the poem not more appropriate, more realistic — more truth-bearing? The TV glamour girl who gives us factual details about a new floor wax or cigarette filter may be endowed with romantic attraction; but in the realms of our *essential living*, she retains an aura of mediocrity. On the other hand, the family doctor who really cares is fear and hope and sorrow and dying mixed with joy; he is the truth-bearer, and the dignity we bestow upon him declares it.

Or, regard CHILDHOOD by Marcia Masters and compare it with the romantic poem we just examined.

> For sound we had the wagon wheels
> Exchanging anecdotes;
> Apples that spring from trees,
> Lamenting softly as they hit the ground;
> And wind that left
> A frail applause among the pines.
>
> For color — there was sudden rain
> Shaken like gooseberries from the sky,
> And sunset loosing
> Its untidy circus in the west.
>
> And, Oh, the scents
> Homely, and wonderful,
> Of rancid apples draining in the sand,
> Of sassafras and woodpiles
> With their lonely smell of dew.
>
> Then there was winter,
> When hallways ached with darkness,
> And the grate burned down to a desolate glitter
> As the cold sun reckoned with a world of snow.

First, Marcia Masters dares to say "frail applause." "Frail" has negative connotations. The romantic, the traditional poet would not use it to speak of a scene that is meant to be precious and close, attractive enough to linger over. But how precisely right the image is! It is frail because it is among pines, which give a thin, light sound; but, even more so, it is frail because it is the wind of childhood, the longed-for time, and all that is beautiful in that far, enchanted land is more elusive, thin, and evanescent, dies away more swiftly in proportion to our desire that it persist.

And who would think of rain "shaken like gooseberries from the sky"? Not the more usual, acceptable poet, not the stylist of the grand manner. What a ridiculous comparison! But that is why it is effective here: the child would certainly find it anything but logical; his dreaming, leaping, rainbowing mind would make it into almost anything desirable.

And the same with "sunset loosing / its untidy circus in the west." Not a well-ordered picture. Not a reassuring or respectably romantic one. But circuses are untidy. And sunsets can be filled with the hurly-burly of great, wild, awesome color exactly like the scramble and riot of the big show, that most stupendous marvel in a child's life.

And what does the word "draining" do? It brings up a sense of loss, dying, suffering — a negative and bitter sense. Not the neat fillip or the clean, brisk perfume of the poetry most beloved by all; but it hits home: in just that way a child would feel the experience of apples, rancid, losing their life and sweetness which he, the child, might keep and taste. The terror, wonder, and painful sorrow of such an experience would utilize just such an unromantic word "draining" — just as the heart's blood of a companion dog drains out on the wet asphalt where he lies, convulsed, hit by a car.

Then, in modern verse, there are the images that hit with

even greater impact, in a rapid, furious kind of elation. Judah M. Turkat, in FACES BEFORE writes:

> Adam, deprived by God
> Left scars on the wings of pheasants,
> Glazed and dazed the hearts of the rocks,
> Revoked the prisms in the lightning flashes
> And muffled the thunder with clouds of lime.
> For Eve, the earth quaked and filled the fields
> And ravines with fire and flood.
> The giant oaks split their trunks
> And gasped for air like throat slit cocks.

The "scars on the wings of pheasants," the dazed hearts of rocks: we might call this the noiseless pneumatic drill of modern verse; it opens wells of understanding even as it cuts and pains. "Throat slit cocks." An unappetizing picture. A sentiment not fashionable in the verse columns of daily uplift, but bringing home with a fresh sting the violence and terror of Adam's tragedy.

There are, of course, poets who distort their own progressive talents, and in effect harm legitimate modern work; there are some who sound the abrasive call of the extremist. In the vernacular, they are the screwballs or the faddists. They have failed to balance the outreachings of *now* with soundness of the past's poetic wisdom; they have failed to mate the plane's wingspread to the heft of the fuselage.

Chris Bjerknes is a contemporary poet who has done much fine work, but consider the imagery in these lines from the poem APRIL:

> the jay gouge the eye
> of wind, the simple shrieks of wren that blister
> the silence, the chilled spider rattling in

mad delirium spindling toward dust
the wind splitting
                    his web,
                              the multiple mirrors
fallen in the coffee mud reflecting the universe
under the rubbery fog stretched over the sweepings
of dust and lampswinging the dark from crowds
and mobs thighing down the avenue at the broken
elbows of time, I shall ply my way
breaking loaves of the calloused moon
gather the minnowed fishes of light
          the wind becomes the epitaph
why then, shall I be
                    brief in the blue empty coffin of
crying heaven, where the wet wind blows
the jaundiced eye of the goat like the dunes
shifting their poise, the pines
nibbling at the sea's hem, neither the blown
muscled maidens whistling nor the scraping
of the dolphin's spine, nor the old woman waiting
here the sleevish gutter of the flesh
the spawning toads, like a child with the moss
of night and memory hung on the moon's indistinct
laughter breaking nightingales across the night's
back, the faith that no faith is taught, nor
properly disseminated, the moon's cheek shaken . . .

Do all these images add up to anything? They are caco-
phonous, divergent, discordant, for no reason whatsoever. It
is like the flailing of a loose connecting-rod in oil grown
too thin. "The multiple mirrors / fallen in the coffee mud,"
"rubbery fog stretched over the sweepings / of dust," "breaking loaves of the calloused moon," "the jaundiced eye of the
goat like the dunes / shifting their poise," "the scraping / of
the dolphin's spine," "memory hung on the moon's indistinct

/ laughter" — these have the sound of ranting. What connection is there between the mirrors and the coffee mud, the loaves and the callouses on the moon? New, jagged images and concepts are hurled in with the abandon of an arsonist heaping furniture on a fire. Where is the pattern, the undergirding logic, the touching upon the coherence of life which lies beneath all chaos?

It is an exercise of the ego — imagery for the sake of imagining, to astound, to overwhelm. Apart from the mangled effects of the whole, each shred by itself is dabbled with needless gore. "The scraping / of the dolphin's spine" is merely ludicrous. Scraping in what context, and why? "Memory hung on the moon's indistinct / laughter." Even if memory could be imagined hanging on the moon, who would want to go even further and try to visualize not the moon merely, but an appendage to it, a sort of vestigial organ called "indistinct laughter," and then drape that memory made into some kind of ectoplasm onto the astonishing ectoplasmic organ of the indistinct laughter projecting from the moon?

Modern poetry is blunt, unprecedented; it deals in fragmentation and shock, but the *genuine* avant-garde poet avoids such gibberish, for its effect is to undermine true experiment, to jeopardize his development. Little wonder, he may conclude, that so many readers are baffled by modern poetry.

The virtue of much "beat" poetry is its vitality. It is spontaneous and virile; its images and ideas have a cutting edge which leaves the pain of recognition. But again what about discipline, the controls that have always been inherent in the finest art now or in the past? Let us look at the first half of Allen Ginsberg's poem, DEATH TO VAN GOGH'S EAR:

Poet is Priest

Money has reckoned the soul of America

Congress broken thru to the precipice of Eternity

the President built a War machine which will vomit and rear
    up Russia out of Kansas

The American Century betrayed by a mad Senate which no
    longer sleeps with its wife

Franco has murdered Lorca the fairy son of Whitman

just as Mayakovsky committed suicide to avoid Russia

Hart Crane distinguished Platonist committed suicide to wave
    in the wrong America

just as millions of tons of human wheat were burned in secret
    caverns under the White House

while India starved and screamed and ate mad dogs full
    of rain

and mountains of eggs were reduced to white powder in the
    halls of Congress

no godfearing man will walk there again because of the stink
    of the rotten eggs of America

and the Indians of Chiapas continue to gnaw their vitaminless
    tortillas

aborigines of Australia perhaps gibber in the eggless wilderness

and I rarely have an egg for breakfast tho my work requires
    infinite eggs to come to birth in Eternity

eggs should be eaten or given to their mothers

and the grief of the countless chickens of America is expressed
    in the screaming of her comedians over the radio

Detroit has built a million automobiles of rubber trees and
    phantoms

but I walk, I walk, and the Orient walks with me, and all
    Africa walks

and sooner or later North America will walk

for as we have driven the Chinese Angel from our door he will
    drive us from the Golden Door of the future

we have not cherished pity on Tanganyika

Einstein alive was mocked for his heavenly politics

Bertrand Russell driven from New York for getting laid
and the immortal Chaplin has been driven from our shores
   with the rose in his teeth
a secret conspiracy by Catholic Church in the lavatories of
   Congress has denied contraceptives to the unceasing
   masses of India.
Nobody publishes a word that is not the cowardly robot rav-
   ings of a depraved mentality
the day of the publication of the true literature of the American body will be the day of Revolution
the revolution of the sexy lamb
the only bloodless revolution that gives away corn
poor Genet will illuminate the harvesters of Ohio
Marijuana is a benevolent narcotic but J. Edgar Hoover
   prefers his deathly scotch
And the heroin of Lao-Tze & the Sixth Patriarch is punished
   by the electric chair
but the poor junkies have nowhere to lay their heads
fiends in our government have invented a cold-turkey cure
   for addiction as obsolete as the Defense Early Warning
   Radar System.
I am the defense early warning radar system
I see nothing but bombs
I am not interested in preventing Asia from being Asia
and the government of Russia and Asia will rise and fall but
   Asia and Russia will not fall
I doubt if anyone will ever fall anymore except governments
fortunately all the governments will fall
the only ones which won't fall are the good ones
and the good ones don't yet exist.

What is the effect here? There is a powerful sweep of
emotion; ideas that are sharp and relentless; images —
"while India starved and screamed and ate mad dogs full
of rain / and mountains of eggs were reduced to white pow-

der in the halls of Congress" — individually, bold and effective. But the total impression, the impact, is one of diffusion. Of course, by the impetuosity and chaos of his diction, the poet may be conveying the madness of our day which he inveighs against, but would not more control carry his effects much better? The poem rapidly spreads into prose, in such lines as, "and I rarely have an egg for breakfast tho my work requires infinite eggs to come to birth in Eternity / eggs should be eaten or given to their mothers." The poet knows how to avoid the trite phrase or picture, but the line lengths, the structure, and the tone are loose. The impact is vitiated throughout because there is no discernible discipline beyond the avoidance of the cliché in word, idea, and image. This is an achievement in itself, but it is not enough. Even this breaks down in such phrases as "the Golden Door of the future," or "the cowardly robot cravings of a depraved mentality / the day of the publication of the true literature of the American body will be the day of Revolution."

While there is energy and conviction and power in the new "beat" verse, and while it has brought fresh infusions to contemporary poetry, its exponents tend toward disorder and self-indulgence. Now and then, Ginsberg, Ferlinghetti, and others of the avant-garde, mostly in their shorter, more economical efforts, do exercise controls, with magically superior results. The poem we have just read, however, is more typical and illustrates the weaknesses and virtues of "beat poetry." The more traditional poets of today surpass much of the new freer borderland poetry in this one respect — discipline of language.

Let us look again at one of the poets of the avant-garde whose work we criticized earlier in this section. AFTER LOVE by Chris Bjerknes:

the breath lines the lea, over there
boned round the clawing veins of light as
to nerve, then proud the cry of wind,
the lea-tongued grass woven as it seems
in the rope of breath, the grown roots
wired deep in time

the hammerheaded drunkard
jay, breaks the emerald memory, and
the grass shadows drive through
the hand, twists, long legged
birds wade for worms, the dusk bleeding
and evening came opened the shell
of shadow from its flowered pain

the pale fingered moon places softly
the damp dream of the seas lips
on his, and drowned he sleeps.

Compare this poem to Bjerknes' APRIL. Why is this the more successful poem? Here, there is continuity, control, a hard pure clear strength. Not only is it a fine poem, a far cry from the other example, but it illustrates another element of modern imagery: the piling up of pictures apparently disconnected but all adding up to a tangency, an aura — each image presented without formal statement. There is not a full grammatical cementing of each image into the context, but there is cohesion of mood: the images create a sort of relationship of their own, without benefit of literal clarity.

In this kind of verse there is something left to our imagination; we can do some of the work for ourselves — just as an abstract painting may give us a sense of participation-through-discovery-by-ourselves. We might feel good after reading an explicit old-fashioned poem because it flatters our preconceptions, encourages our tendency to believe what is easy to understand. But great artistic enjoyment means work as well as emotional reflex. Good poems grow on us, through a second and third, a fourth and fifth reading.

The images in AFTER LOVE develop a relationship and meaning by virtue of their cohesive emotion and total impact. The spice, or fillip, referred to earlier when we examined the individual image, must also be present with the series of images — the elusiveness, as natural a part of any truth as the stereo is natural in a modern living-room. But mainly, there is something *creative* that has to be done by the reader — like the man at a Thanksgiving feast, who, prodding about in a bowl of nuts, finds the choicest half-opened prizes, cracks them, and extracts the clean, moist meat. The more traditional verse gives us the nuts all extracted, salted, and in a bag.

In AFTER LOVE, notice how the images form implication, an emanation of meaning as we go along. The thoughts are not bound by orderly, formal statement; they are allowed to build their own dynamism and context. As John Ciardi put it once, "each poem must make a life of its own."

Consider the images. "Boned" is a far remove from "clawing veins of light," and both are apparently quite unrelated to "proud the cry of wind." But combine them, and we see the poet is trying to give us gradually a sense of exultance, aliveness, awareness — the whole anatomy of the body felt exquisitely after love, the lover proudly aware of it and transferring its qualities to the earth. The strong, gratified breathing ("the breath lines the lea") becomes identified with grass and meadows, the bones with the structure of the land which enfolds light, just as bones anchor certain nerves — nerves that are stretched and eager, as those of lovers are; the proud tempo of blood is transferred to wind.

"The grown roots / wired deep in time" flashes another

impulse on the screen of the poem, inferring that the act of love is like nature, rooted deep in immemorial habit and heritage. And the "hammerheaded drunken jay" — drunken as the soul of the lover might be drunk with fulfillment and wild peace. The dusk "bleeding" suggests their pleasure and gratitude are as poignant as bleeding; "flowered pain" implies again the pagan brutal sweetness of love's paradox — the end of what seems timeless.

All this adds up to mood, general impact at the end of the poem; all the subterranean effects break through to give weight to the final emotion.

Yes, glancing back at the two earlier examples preceding AFTER LOVE, we must admit that at times contemporary poetry is vulnerable to attack from the traditionally minded. But, we have to thank those who have indulged in excess, also: they broke the ground. Just as James Joyce contributed the first stream-of-consciousness technique — so labored that few read it at the time, yet giving rise to modified and lasting forms — so out of the excessive fragmentation and explosiveness of much modern imagery comes the controlled finesse of the superior modern poet, who turns the stream-of-consciousness method to whole and lasting effect.

Turn for a moment to THAT UNDERGROUND SUN by Felix N. Stefanile:

That underground sun that warms my feet
shines where Jacob's Ladder slants to the sea
and the cobblestones reveal me turtles brave.
I have come to a goodly meet-
ing among the rosemary, the phlox and the peony.

That underground sun shoots forth a river of claws
in the meadow, with a whirlpool at my ears,

but slow the wind flows, and there are no flaws
in the big blue air where I am a swimmer
gracefully floating from year to year.

But I feel the claw and crab and funny cancer
pulling with tide-pull long from Venus to Maine,
and the sun burns at my flesh with the nip of a pincer.
Retrieve me, seas, where under the ground, sun reigns
and my bones' coral morrows will glow like a stain.

That underground sun gives me the lowtide blues
for a squirrel drowned in the spring, or white in the
	winter.
The sharks are flopping in the chimney-flues,
and the lake upstairs floats one long cloud
serene and still like a submarine hunter.

Oh Davey Jones is chirping in the arbor
and I shall have passage after his last swallows.
That underground sun is drowning in the tall waters,
and the tides are rip, and ripe the snails in the shallows,
and the King and Queen are wet, and their sons and
	daughters.

This poem is concerned not so much with the obvious and
literal as with the essence of experience. What is the poet
saying here and how do his images help give us this essence?

Take the third stanza: "The sun burns at my flesh with the
nip of a pincer." The under-sea life nips him, takes him with
its wondrous strong creatures as the above-ground sun would
smart him with the pincers of a sunburn. We feel, we accept
his substitution: the under-sea, the underground, *is now* the
world of sunlight and sky.

Then, next: "Retrieve me, seas, where under the ground,
sun reigns / and my bones' coral morrows will glow like a

stain." The bones compare to coral, glowing through all future time with the wild, miraculous underground sky-and-sun where "there are no flaws / in the big blue air" and "where I am a swimmer / gracefully floating from year to year"; and "like a stain" — the words make us feel that life has been shed with glad fulfillment, merged with all loveliness.

The sun and sky, which we all know and love, then, exists where we'd least of all expect it — underground, undersea. Beauty lives in paradox; beauty is an inverted world. All of us *feel* that this is true; that good is in the heart of the ruffian and beggar; that love rustles in the bracken of the criminal's intent; that death conceals an astonishing life. Isn't that what the poem gives us most of all — this supreme concept of beauty? It is conventional to think that the sun is only aboveground; but the poet says it is beneath land and water too; it is conventional to think that beauty is only in the life we can see, feel, analyze about us; but the poet says we'll find it in the hidden, the unnavigable, the most impossible depths that will never be plumbed. This premonition, this psychic experience we all have, that beauty is paradoxical in a thousand ways, is reduced finally to the sense that darkness and death are but deception, and contains perhaps the truest delight of all.

Now Stefanile does not try to control and direct the expression of his idea — he does not deliberately plant it for us the way the owners of public fishponds stock their ponds with fish and then charge the public to come in and catch the helpless creatures and fry them at assembly-line fireplaces. Rather, he takes us up a forest-girded stream, through rugged country where our joy is measured by the love of equal battle, cunning, patience, and the quarry we conquer at last has a courage and tenacity we admire.

Stefanile uses the stream-of-consciousness technique to ex-

cellent effect, presenting his material in an *apparently* un-
organized series of images, connected by association. Through
his skillful handling, the poem becomes more spontaneous,
diffused, and flexible.

Just as the cigarette after hard labor and food is the essence
of smoking; as the act of love is the essence of the many
hours of touch and glance and casual word that precede it —
so the imagery of the modern poet cuts through to underlying,
elementary meaning.

And finally, the image of more contemporary verse takes
as its subject-matter the stuff of the present-day world. First
of all, the personal and subjective themes in poetry — love
and yearning, loss and recollection — which long have been
associated with the romantic, receive now the bright searching
of the commonplace. We are made aware of reality through
the things that are incorrigibly vernacular and real all about
us: the objects that sear our flesh and clutter our pores and
yet sustain us, that are our very selves — the lovely things
found in the shape of what we are, not what we have been.
Listen to Richard Wilbur's A Simile for Her Smile:

> Your smiling, or the hope, the thought of it,
> Makes in my mind such pause and abrupt ease
> As when the highway bridgegates fall,
> Balking the hasty traffic, which must sit
> On each side massed and staring, while
> Deliberately the drawbridge starts to rise:
> Then horns are hushed, the oilsmoke rarefies,
> Above the idling motors one can tell
> The packet's smooth approach, the slip,
> Slip of the silken river past the sides,
> The ringing of clear bells, the dip
> And slow cascading of the paddle wheel.

Have you ever seen before a eulogy to one's love mixed elegantly and eloquently with traffic horns and rarefied oilsmoke? It recalls Spender's poem about the train, which creates out of the mechanical and prosaic a thing of supernal loveliness. Here is a subject traditionally wreathed in the roses of "acceptable" romantic idiom and image — nature, the sweet, reposeful, and undisturbing — that in Wilbur's poem takes fire from the sordid material stuff, the *hereness,* of our environment.

Often, the modern image is characterized by the telescoping and skimping of syntax to achieve the staccato flavor of the present-day world; avoidance of the literal and formal for the implied; the oblique; and the shock, or abrupt effect, in and of itself and in the total structure of the poem.

All these traits of the modern image are equally applicable to modern diction out of which imagery, the primary element of poetry, is created. Let us take a single piece to demonstrate how the two are superimposed upon each other, or are nearly synonymous in definition. Here are the first seven stanzas of THE MARIONETTES by Felix N. Stefanile:

> See how they dream their wooden dreams:
> oak legends are in their painted eyes.
> Their ardor is of crepe and chalk.
> The fire is their only surprise.
>
> Catch how they mouth their gargoyle talk;
> they even love with a scratching sound.
> The fire is their only surprise,
> Pinocchio burning himself to the ground.
>
> Watch how they dance their clacking dance;
> their kiss is like the breaking of a box.
> They would sprout leaves like fingers of sense —
> Master Gepetto, how they dance.

Sauntering past with chirping knees
through the proscenium's feast of eyes,
wanting, perhaps, not to be made of wood.
The fire is their only surprise.

City of iron metaphors,
the children applaud their angular pranks
as their freak noses bump in fiction.
Do they hope that mothers will offer thanks?

See how they turn their necks of bark,
wound and wired for noise and friction.
They are not muddy children lost in the dark.
The fire is their only surprise.

Friend Cricket, your ardent piccolo
weeps from the wall like a prophecy.
They are so lonely racked upon the shelves.
They can weep splinters if only they try.

Take the word "clacking." It is not of itself an image, as
"cup of the body" was an image in AFTER ILLNESS, or the
whole picture of sharks flopping in the chimney flues in THAT
UNDERGROUND SUN. It is an adjective, part of the para-
phernalia by which we get the picture of the dance; yet without it, we would have no image. Its effectiveness makes the
image effective. "Clacking" could not be improved upon; it
gives the sound of a marionette with precise perfection. But
it is not essentially an example of "modern" diction; it might
well have appeared in a poem by any poet of the twenties, or
even before.

Notice the poet's choice of another word: "chirping." This,
again, is diction, not a full image. But it is modern diction,
that makes the impact of the entire two-line image successful.

It is an original, courageous word; it has a healthy everyday-ness: although not a machine-age word, it is strong, simple, highly connotative. It is not elite, or common to conventional poetry — unless used in reference to crickets or birds; in any connection such as knees, it would be too harsh and crude.

Then, the *force* of "chirping." Unexpected, a bit of an electric shock. Ordinarily, who would associate "chirping" with knees? But these are wooden knees, and, if they brushed together, they would make a plaintive sound; and in the context of the whole poem, with its references to pathetic Pinocchio, the sound of the knees bending and brushing — awkwardly, ungovernably, oversmoothed from weary effort — the idea of plaintiveness and stridency conveyed by "chirping" would be especially appropriate.

Moreover, "chirping" jars a bit in its context; the words around it are all rather pleasant, innocuous, soft: "dance," "sauntering past," "through the proscenium's feast of eyes." Customary, and easy to take. Then the word "chirping." Startling. But exact. Though risking itself on boldness and surprise, it is truthful.

Yet, it cannot quite be considered an image itself; it is diction. The effect, however, is identical with that of image. We feel the whole nature and meaning of the knees because we hear the chirping; the complete picture is almost that one word. The diction, or selected word here, therefore, bearing the marks of modern tendency, can be said to be very much the same thing as imagery. There is superimposition, a sameness akin to identity.

3

Rhythm and Sound

IMAGE AND DICTION are bound up with the rhythm and sound which carry them. The ductile quality of the whole poem is dependent on how these four elements are strung and balanced. Image can be victorious only if the rhythm or sound patterns are appropriate to it; diction determines the musical note struck.

First, let us consider the more traditional type of metre (that is, the sound, or stress-measurements, of the line) and music. For centuries we have associated poetry, fundamental poetry, with the lyric, with its musical and romantic connotations. Verse, we have felt, should sing; it should have cadence and melody, and sift into the heart like gold sifting through the boughs of elms to greensward. There are many who still feel this way, and it is true that much good poetry still depends upon these attributes. For example, witness HONEY FROM THE LION, by Leah Bodine Drake:

I came upon it unaware. . . .
First there was sand and silence there,
Blue-burning haze and scorching rock,
Short-daggered grass . . . and then the shock
Of great limbs stretched before a lair:

The old brave body, stiff and prone,
Of some king-lion done to death
Upon the threshold of his earth,
All that huge ardor still as stone.

Wild bees had built their honeycomb
In his bright carcass, thunder-maned.
Through brow and jaw the nectar strained:
What Pharoah in his spicy tomb
Had such rich amber seal his mouth?

I dipped my fingers in the sweet
And oh! the fiery savage meat
Bred from the lands of lack and drouth
Tanged with wild joy and deep unrest
And desolate courage and the strength
Of loneliness: I knew at length
What fury burned in Samson's breast!

Now garden honey's overmild
To satisfy the sharpened taste
Of one who's eaten of the Waste.
I know a hunger never filled
Since that strange banquet long ago,
That dark and bitter sweetness grown
Out of the lion's blood and bone,
Out of the desert's pride and woe.

Now the metre and over-all structure of this poem are not
precise and formal throughout — that is, the rhymes have
varying patterns. But the beat is the regular tetrameter (four

feet to the line) — a metre suitable here because, usually, it can drive home emotion and color with greater efficacy than the pentameter (since the pentameter, more sober and deliberate — with five feet to the line — is better fitted for the contemplative and cerebral), and the rhymes, though there are such slant effects as "overmild" and "filled," would fall into the category of the traditional, close rhyme.

The euphony is clear and pleasant throughout: "I dipped my fingers in the sweet," "Bred from the lands of lack and drouth" — graduated vowel sound, alliteration, rounded assonance — traits of our best lyrical heritage. Moreover, the syntax is complete, though there is compression and incisiveness; and there is none of the jitterbugging, circus-diving, barrel-jumping, none of the chasms in structure, meaning, grammar, which appear in much contemporary verse. Therefore, it is an example of the long-established: an extremely powerful poem written with the rhythm and sound of the finest in the more traditional stream of the art. It is primarily a poem of image — haunting, and of essentially emotional impact — though there is very definite and provocative philosophical understatement.

To show how established rhyme patterns can contain and enhance another species as well — the idea poem, which is unreservedly philosophic — let us take Donald Babcock's Two Things:

> Two things were set
> That I must learn
> On earth, though tears be wet
> And fire unstinting burn.
> Seek through the flesh: you will not find
> The living likeness of the mind;
> Explore the mind: you will discern no trace
> Of matter or its clinging shell of space.

This learned, pass on, and presently confess
That nerves lend action to your willfulness.
The boundaries of self evade
The searching of your careful blade.
Even to the very end,
And each by each refined,
The two will blend:
The flesh, the mind.

Notice here at once the flexibility of the rhyme schemes, from dimeter (two feet to the line) to pentameter, and from pentameter back to dimeter. Through them, most efficaciously, the thought content is shaped and dispatched. But, observe the couplet-rhyming throughout, close in cadence and by and large with end-stopped lines. The punchlines at the end are superb; nothing other than a close, pronounced beat and rhyme would do, of course; but the fact remains that the over-all handling of the poem, in its structural and musical arrangement, is conventional.

This does not mean it is not a good poem; in fact, it is a fine poem indeed. But we would not classify it as modern.

What then would be modern in this particular respect — in respect to pattern of sound?

One of the first and most obvious points about the newer poetry is that metre and sound operate in less regular ways: the metre may be very uneven, often jagged. This contributes to the general impressionistic effect: also, in any given constellation of vowel and consonant sounds, it acts as a comet of dramatic impulse and contrast, the excitement of the erratic. Let us note how this can be brought about unobtrusively, with a deft hand; and since we have been discussing the pictorial and the contemplative as two different emphases, let us take a verse in which there is *both* strong imagery and emotive-

impact *and* an undergirding of philosophy — DEAD WASP
by Kenneth Alling:

> The small wasp lies in state,
> A formidable design in black and gold:
> Tiered like a Chinese tower, his abdomen;
> His wings as hyaline as heaven,
> Windows the now elegiac light pours through.

First, we notice the unevenness of the metre: 3, 5, 5, 3, 5.
Next, the lack of similar sound in the end-words: "state,"
"gold," "abdomen," "heaven," "through." There are none
of the long-accepted rhyme effects, full, half, or slant. In fact,
the impression is one of dissonance. Note, for example, that
word "abdomen." What an awkward word to leave one with
at the finish of an end-stopped line. A plural-syllable or a
feminine-rhyme word at the conclusion of a line is always a
bit risky anyway; here, the word "abdomen," tossed in cava-
lierly, is disconcerting to one not accustomed to modern poetry.

The point is, then, that the exact rhythm is not as important
to the new poet *as the meaning or sense*. He does not tie
himself to the rocket of identical sound *per se* and hurl himself
into the black stratosphere of his poem, willy-nilly. He may
release a rocket of true-beat, or off-beat music, however he
may feel; his chief aim is to enjoy and savor, to register alle-
giance to the demands of the moment, the dictates of thought
as it emerges in the given line or stanza.

There are some of the more conventional effects in DEAD
WASP: alliteration: "tiered like a Chinese tower"; "hyaline
as heaven"; and assonance: "small wasp." But the clap of
the bell-tongue is due to the weight of *spontaneity* rather than
close form; to involuntary sound, rather than the guided and
closeted. The modern poet wishes, in his rhythms and metres,
to be liberated, spontaneously whole. The most honest thought

dwells below the surface of form and too-conscious cerebration. He wishes to tap the vein, to aid the uprush of the unconscious. A complete adherence to full rhyme and exact formula would bind and inhibit him.

Finally, in looking over DEAD WASP, we find that the philosophy is bound in faithfully with the image, infuses the climax lines and draws to the fore the implication of the preceding. His death suggests the whole range of religious argument, belief, and wonder. Perhaps he has as much right to the dignity of proper burial ceremony as man; he is transported to the realm of his ancestors, maybe, as fittingly as any Chinese dead; and his hyaline (transparent) wings become the glass through which the very light of heaven's grace now shines.

And how does the informal, non-euphonious metre and sound aid the theme and total impact of the poem? Take the last line. It is a long line; its vowel and consonant relationships are not melodious. Just enunciate the vowels alone in that line, in the order in which they come: there is a wide range (the mark of dissonance): the last "oo" sound of "through" is particularly off-key with the preceding notes. Then, the whole line has a matter-of-factness about it, a conversational everydayness which clashes with the regal, elevated atmosphere which comes before. And the line is drawn out to five feet, which gives it a slower, more prosaic bulk.

The poem simultaneously bows in humility with the dead wasp and raises him to what we normally consider the sublime. Unadorned and commonplace language startles us with a challenge that is democratic; rhythm and sound reduced to the ordinary help us to feel the willingness of Deity to descend in pity and illumine the least of his creatures.

Where the tone of the traditional poem was apt to be more

formal and elevated, even declamatory, modern poetry —
perhaps as much as anything else — brings metre and tonal
quality close to the vernacular, the conversational idiom.
Galway Kinnell illustrates this in To WILLIAM CARLOS WIL-
LIAMS (AFTER A LECTURE AT A SCHOOL OF ENGLISH):

> When you came and you talked and you read with your
> Private zest from the varicose marble
> Of the podium, the lovers of literature
> Paid you the real tribute of their almost total
> Inattention — although one woman when you spoke of a pig
> Did squirm, and it is only fair to report another gig-
> gled. But you didn't even care. You seemed
> Above remarking we were not your friends.
> You hung around inside the rimmed
> Circles of your heavy glasses and smiled and
> So passed a lonely evening. In an hour
> Of talking your honesty built you a tower.
>
> When it was over and you sat down and the chair-
> man got up and smiled and congratulated
> You and shook your hand, I watched a professor
> In neat bow tie and enormous tweeds, who patted
> A faint praise of the sufficiently damned,
> Drained spittle from his pipe, then scrammed.

First of all, "When you came and you talked and you read"
gives one the sense of the flow of life, activity, informality; the
repetition of "you" would be unnecessary in a tight, nicely
metrical line — but a person spontaneously talking would
throw in the extra "you's," perhaps for emphasis.

Next, "varicose marble" is something of a mild shock; it
pops a little firecracker of humor at the beginning, natural,
off-hand, unpretentious. Here we have no smug attitude, no

traditional poetic serenity; everything goes. The word "zest" next to "varicose" gives the flavor of the incongruity and irony of life in general, this scene in particular.

Then, the lines throughout are far from being end-stopped or blandly run-on in the manner of more traditional verse; instead, they use a run-on bluntness that is jolting. Note "varicose marble / of the podium." That "of the podium" beginning a line is like a face-on collision with a door, or a paper bag being whacked, especially when tucked in between the nice classical word "marble," which we associate with Greek parthenons, and the very bland and deliberately hackneyed phrase "lovers of literature."

The sound is doing something: the awkward metre is adding up to the jumpy, contorted disgust of the author for hothouse culture. It is taking broken, spotty, disjointed cadence and word-tone, and appropriating them to the job of giving the *real* scene, the way it would be — not some dream concept or an apotheosis of a phase of living. Regard that run-on effect: "total / inattention." Nothing is clumsier than an adjective cut off from its noun like this, a whole line away. It gives the word "inattention" great stress, even to a ludicrous extent.

There are other jolting effects. To create a rhyme for "pig" the word "giggled" is deftly sundered, and lo! we have "gig-" as the appropriate sound. And later, "chairman" is torn apart at the end of a line (a projection, perhaps, of the subconscious wish of the author — another argument, maybe, for the use of the eruptive subconscious in modern poetry!)

And above all, the sound of that last word in the poem, "scrammed." Unsqueamish and bluff as an old sea-captain. "Scrammed." There is your slang word, your down-to-earth word, that carries the temper and cant of the crowd. One sees the haste, the indecorous furtiveness and finality of that scene.

It would be impossible to understand the tempo and music of modern poetry without speaking again of Gerard Manley Hopkins and his influence. What he has done with his sprung rhythm is to quicken and intensify the beat of verse. Some feel that his technique imparts a plethora of image and hard sound, a kind of clumsy blundering violence. But there is no doubt that his contribution to prosody is as great as any in the last century. Let us observe the first lines of his GOD'S GRANDEUR:

The world is charged with the grandeur of God.
It will flame out, like shining from shook foil;
It gathers to a greatness, like the ooze of oil
Crushed. Why do men then now not reck his rod?
Generations have trod, have trod, have trod;
And all is seared with trade; bleared, smeared with toil;
And wears man's smudge and shares man's smell; the soil
Is bare now, nor can foot feel, being shod.
And for all this, nature is never spent.

Consider the fourth line: "Crushed. Why do men then now not reck his rod?" Now, in poetry, as we know, the natural metric rise and fall, the emphasis, depends upon meaning. Where the meaning is obviously emphatic, the syllable is stressed. What Hopkins does is to cram a great many accented syllables into one line. "Crushed" certainly requires emphasis. The strong interrogative "why" must be accented. And to get the full import and drive, the complete value of indignation, all the words from "men" through "reck" must bear the weight of stressed sound. Try reading the line and letting up on the word "then," or permitting the word "now" to go unaccented. "Not" must be leaned on vigorously for clarity, to undergird the poet's mood of astonishment. And then the last word, "rod," is accented. Thus, in the whole line of ten syllables, only two, represented by the words "do" and "his," can be considered mild in nature and meaning, permitting any let-up. And even "his" could be thought of as needing emphasis, for it contrasts Deity's might, *His* might, with man's.

Or take the ninth line: "Is bare now, nor can foot feel, being shod." Is it not impossible to get the usual regular cadence out of the line? — impossible to establish traditional metre, because there are so many accented words and syllables? There is no neat, pleasant rise and fall from unimportant words to important, forceful ones, and back again. Almost all of the words must be credited with a major role in the line. Only "is," "can," and "being" could conceivably be minimized. That means that out of nine syllables, six are accented, and only three unaccented.

By this method, poetry becomes more surcharged, triphammer; and much verse today is shot through with Hopkins' influence. INERTIA by Audrey McGaffin will serve as an example:

Nothing wild —
and woolly fog
enfolds this game, clogged
with a lull and a yawn
and a lukewarm luck
that warms no bones.

The dirty
dog-eared back
of the day, like a card
cast from the deck,
lies on the lake,
and its two-spot eyes
stare at the sky
but take in no trick.

45

The doldrums
have dealt this deuce
of a dull day.

Note the words "enfolds this game, clogged." Out of five syllables, four are accented. Only the "en" of "enfolds" eases up. "Lukewarm luck" and "warms no bones" have to be emphasized, as do "dirty / dog-eared back." And the total number of lesser words, conjunctions, articles, pronouns, is small. The poet seeks a harder and more effective impact; and observe how the short lines aid the triphammer metrics, the mood of laconic, sordid dejection.

Or let us consider this poem by Dylan Thomas, IF I WERE TICKLED BY THE RUB OF LOVE:

If I were tickled by the rub of love,
A rooking girl who stole me for her side,
Broke through her straws, breaking my bandaged string,
If the red tickle as the cattle calve
Still set to scratch a laughter from my lung,
I would not fear the apple nor the flood
Nor the bad blood of spring.

Shall it be male or female? say the cells,
And drop the plum like fire from the flesh.
If I were tickled by the hatching hair,
The winged bone that sprouted in the heels,
The itch of man upon the baby's thigh,
I would not fear the gallows nor the axe
Nor the crossed sticks of war.

Shall it be male or female? say the fingers
That chalk the walls with green girls and their men.
I would not fear the muscling-in of love
If I were tickled by the urchin hungers

Rehearsing heat upon a raw-edged nerve.
I would not fear the devil in the loin
Nor the outspoken grave.

If I were tickled by the lovers' rub
That wipes away not crow's-foot nor the lock
Of sick old manhood on the fallen jaws,
Time and the crabs and the sweethearting crib
Would leave me cold as butter for the flies,
The sea of scums could drown me as it broke
Dead on the sweethearts' toes.

This world is half the devil's and my own,
Daft with the drug that's smoking in a girl
And curling round the bud that forks her eye.
An old man's shank one-marrowed with my bone,
And all the herrings smelling in the sea,
I sit and watch the worm beneath my nail
Wearing the quick away.

And that's the rub, the only rub that tickles.
The knobbly ape that swings along his sex
From damp love-darkness and the nurse's twist
Can never raise the midnight of a chuckle,
Nor when he finds a beauty in the breast
Of lover, mother, lovers, or his six
Feet in the rubbing dust.

And what's the rub? Death's feather on the nerve?
Your mouth, my love, the thistle in the kiss?
My Jack of Christ born thorny on the tree?
The words of death are dryer than his stiff,
My wordy wounds are printed with your hair.
I would be tickled by the rub that is:
Man be my metaphor.

Thomas forces us throughout to read words as accented more frequently than in the usual poem. For example: "I would not fear the apple nor the flood / Nor the bad blood of spring." Only the second syllable of "apple," the three "the's," and "of" can be read as unaccented. The reader is putting stress upon *eleven* syllables and dropping his voice on only five; in the traditional poem there would be a more regular up-and-down cadence. The diction is blunt, hard, Anglo-Saxon — one-syllable words to maintain a vital, high-pitched pace.

In "Nor the crossed sticks of war," all but "the" and "of" must be accented; in "That chalk the walls with green girls and their men," all but "That," "the," and "and." Notice "their," which in the conventional, more metrically exact and swinging line, would go unaccented; but here, the patterns and tone — set up before we arrive — compel us to put stress upon it.

One of the best examples in the poem is the line, "An old man's shank one-marrowed with my bone." Only "an" and "with" go unaccented. And there are ten syllables in the line. "I sit and watch the worm beneath my nail" has ten syllables also; only "and" and "the" are unstressed. Again, in the more conventional line, "my" would demand a drop in the voice. Most intensive of all is the last line, "Man be my metaphor." Every syllable is hard.

Moreover, the kind of concentration of tempo and sound seen in the poems above can accentuate, reinforce the *complete structure of the poem,* and vice versa. For example, let us examine William Carlos Williams' To a Dog Injured in the Street:

48

IT IS MYSELF
>   not the poor beast lying there
>   yelping with pain
that brings me to myself with a start —
>   as at the explosion
>   of a bomb, a bomb that has laid

all the world waste.
>   I can do nothing
>   but sing about it
and so I am assuaged
>   from my pain.

A DROWSY NUMBNESS drowns my sense
>   as if of hemlock
>   I had drunk. I think

of the poetry
>   of René Char
>   and all he must have seen

and suffered
>   that has brought him
>   to speak only of

sedgy rivers,
>   of daffodils and tulips
>   whose roots they water,

even to the freeflowing river
>   that laves the rootlets
>   of those sweet scented flowers

that people the
>   milky
>   way.

49

I REMEMBER *Norma*
    our English setter of my childhood
      her silky ears

and expressive eyes.
    She had a litter
      of pups one night

in our pantry and I kicked
    one of them
      thinking, in my alarm,

that they
    were biting her breasts
      to destroy her.

I REMEMBER also
    a dead rabbit
      lying harmlessly

on the outspread palm
    of a hunter's hand.
      As I stood by

watching
    he took a hunting knife
      and with a laugh

thrust it
    up into the animal's private parts.
      I almost fainted.

WHY SHOULD I think of that now?
    the cries of a dying dog
      are to be blotted out

as best I can.
>René Char
>>you are a poet who believes

in the power of beauty
>to right all wrongs.
>>I believe it also.

With invention and courage
>we shall surpass
>>the pitiful dumb beasts,

let all men believe it,
>as you have taught me also
>>to believe it.

The slant arrangement of the lines is obviously for emphasis, to make the break more definite, to draw out the shock and hesitancy, the deep horror of the experience. Note: "that people the / milky / way." Here are strong, accented words. Broken up this way into separate lines, they aid the contrast, lengthen the sense of aerial beauty as compared to the suffering previously commented on.

The casual, matter-of-fact observations can also be thrown into relief more fittingly against their opposites when the lines are short and hard-hitting. The mood is one of torture, unbearable bitterness, and how much more effective to comment off-handedly:

I REMEMBER, *Norma*
>our English setter of my childhood
>>her silky ears
and expressive eyes.
>She had a litter
>>of pups one night
in our pantry and I kicked
>one of them

than to wax eloquent about it. And then —

> thinking, in my alarm,
> that they
> were biting her breasts
> to destroy her.

Note what the slant arrangement, the compact sound and rhythm can do to make that surprising turn of thought strike home. If the cadence of the lines were extended into tetrameter or pentameter, that would be lost. And the shortening of the lines, the reduction of words, tend to give more compression to them. "To destroy her," for instance, has to be sounded as four accented syllables in this brief, fierce line; but supposing that "that they / were biting her breasts / to destroy her" were written as one tetrameter line. Would it not be difficult in that case to make the "to" and the "de" of "destroy" accented, as well as "her"? It would be necessary to make them unaccented, to give a rise and fall to the whole line, to afford a contrasting softness for the hard syllables such as the "bit-" of "biting" and "breasts." But in the slashed lines, as written, each part looms larger, the mind registers it with greater intensity: thus, the effect is one of stressed syllables only: the sprung rhythm of Hopkins has raised the horsepower of the stanza, and a tighter, sharper beat and sound have aided the staccato form of each stanza and the whole poem.

The same merits are to be found in the lines:

> he took a hunting knife
> and with a laugh
> thrust it
> up into the animal's private parts.
> I almost fainted.

The jerky arrangement puts across the feeling of a spastic agony of remembrance, a reluctance, conflict. The flat, off-hand casualness of "I REMEMBER also / a dead rabbit / lying harmlessly / on the outspread palm / of a hunter's hand" is, first, made more pithy and real by the brief, broken lines, the awkwardness of simple and terrible thought, and second, is thrown into effective relief against the savage horror of those two lines: "thrust it / up into the animal's private parts." "Thrust it" gains from standing alone, and each syllable must be accented; "up into the animal's private parts" is so flat, casual, off-hand that the horror is even more over-whelming — again, understatement and ironic simplicity further the impact of a fresh insight into one of the most complex of subjects: man's bestial cruelty to earth's creatures.

And "I almost fainted." Naked, single, eloquent — re-quiring a force of pronunciation which would be lacking if the words were part of a longer line. Finally, the jagged effect of the form, the metrical variation make the compassion of the mood more profound; for one torn, distracted, and be-wildered by life's ultimate torments would not emote in fluent, regular metre.

Occasionally in modern poetry, in contrast to the spikiness of the pattern just examined, the more regular, time-honored music beat is used to drive home realism; here, a more de-cided cadence adds to the satiric or ironic effect of lines that contemplate life in the essentially realistic, rather than the romantic, manner.

To demonstrate this point, let us take two poems by Walk-er Gibson. First, THAW:

> In time the snowman always dies,
> As even children realize

And do not mourn his sad demise.
In April, when he's long been gone,
And I begin to mow the lawn,
The blades will crack his big black eyes.

Notice the definite recurrence of sound here, very close and meticulous: "dies," "realize," "demise," "eyes." It is like a nursery rhyme in its swing and its rhythm, almost a jingle. The subject being children, this is appropriate; but the inferences and impact are adult; the whimsicality is mixed with a very keen satiric melancholy. "Demise" is a mature word, not the language for the young; a greater effect of contrast and irony is gained by it. The snowman, of course, represents the more pure, unselfconscious pleasures of life, and the poem is a beautiful lesson on growing up — but for the adult, primarily. The blades of the mower are the bitter actualities of change, time. The regularity of sound makes it *seem* like a message for children; the satire and depth of idea, the twist at the end make it a bolt to the heart for the along-in-years. The sound plays a big part in the poem: the contrast between the sound and the underlying serious meaning gives the poem its high voltage.

The naiveté and lightness of the last line conceal a devastating implication: man's dreams get in the way of his practical activities; it is illusory to think that human beings will ever learn to face facts. As long as they live, they will go right on building snowmen (dreaming) and mowing lawns (doing the chores of life) in a hazy realm of incongruity.

The meaning of the poem, says the author, is *intended* largely for elders, though he concludes wistfully that he must despair of imparting awareness. "As even children realize," is, of course, ironic: they do understand, but only in a superficial way; and the inference — note that word "even" — is that adults *don't,* and he's mildly rebuking them. By the end of the poem, we can see that the elder is worse than the child: he will never fully grasp truth.

Or, let us look at another of Gibson's poems, BILLIARDS:

> Late of the jungle, wild and dim,
> Sliced from the elephant's ivory limb,
> Painted, polished, here these spheres
> Rehearse their civilized careers —
> Trapped in a geometric toil,
> Exhibit impact and recoil
> Politely, in a farce of force.
> For this, I utter no remorse
> But praise the complicated plan
> That organizes beast and man
> In pattern so superbly styled
> Late of the jungle, dim and wild.

In the line, "Sliced from the elephant's ivory limb," the assonance of "sliced" and "ivory" is light, casual, matter-of-fact — yet how serious is the operation being performed! Again, effect through contrast. And the elevated, even erudite diction suggests mockingly the "superior" intelligence of man, his evolutionary glory (being able to slice tusks into billiard balls after thousands of years). For example: "Rehearse their civilized careers — / Trapped in a geometric toil." The language becomes academic, just as the distinction man makes between himself and the beast is only a "polite" idea; and the belief that man is advanced is purely an amenity. He thinks he is playing with material he has mastered, but actually, all the time, he is pushing himself around, playing with the stuff of his own nature, fatally.

The word "style" is the giveaway: man's games are only a pretense, a manner and habit evoked, by which he can ra-

55

tionalize and deceive himself. By cleverness he believes he can evade hard truth (just as in THAW, by routine work, mowing the lawn, he believes he can evade it), but he is trapped by futility just as the balls are "trapped in a geometric toil." And the last line, a repetition of the first, clinches the argument: they are both, "beast and man . . . late of the jungle." Therefore, in spite of all deceit, civilized skill, hypocrisy, there is no distinction.

Again, the utter simplicity and directness of the metre, the almost sing-songy effect, carry the complexity with great *ironic* force: the formal or high-falutin' tone of many of the words: "complicated," "geometric," "civilized," "exhibit," accentuate their opposite — the down-to-earth, unscholastic fact of man's self-deception, his unmodified barbarity, represented by his making games from the limbs of other species he can dominate and plunder. The very clash of word-sound now and then furthers the semi-comic effect, the impression of man's bizarre delusions: for example, "Politely, in a farce of force." And the word sounds, the alliterations and assonances, which flow gently together, intensify the sarcasm, the underlying naked gibe — merciless, cold, unadorned: "For *this,* I utter no *remorse* / but praise the com*pl*icated *pl*an," and "In *p*atterns *so* su*p*erbly *st*yled." Or, Ex*h*ibit *impact and* recoil," — a very neat turn of sound in the vowels of the lines; anything but a neat and cordial meaning underneath: man has not maintained the balance of life at all by his depredation — quite the contrary.

Man is urbane, says the outer manner of the poem; he is anything *but,* replies the inner substance: the two are beautifully synchronized.

Lastly, the contemporary poet may turn cadence and sound, through insistent repetition, to more effective use to attack current conventions or injustices. Here is THE ASH AND THE OAK, by Louis Simpson:

When man discovered freedom first
The fighting was on foot,
They were encouraged by their thirst
And promises of loot,
And when it feathered and bows boomed
Their virtue was a root.

Oh, the ash and the oak and the willow tree
And green grows the grass on the infantry!

At Malplaquet and Waterloo
They were polite and proud,
They primed their guns with billets-doux
And, as they fired, bowed.
At Appomattox, too, it seems
Some things were understood.

Oh, the ash and the oak and the willow tree
And green grows the grass on the infantry!

But at Verdun and at Bastogne
There was a great recoil,
The blood was bitter to the bone
The trigger to the soul,
And death was nothing if not dull.
A hero was a fool.

Oh, the ash and the oak and the willow tree
And that's an end of the infantry.

Now repetition has been an aid to the poet from earliest times, in the ballad and other forms, but the intention was usually to obtain a pleasing musical effect — not to convey shock. Could the absurdity of war be conveyed with more delicate virtuosity than in these recurrent sounds and rhythms, the shift at the very end from "And green grows the grass on the infantry" to "And that's an end of the infantry"?

Now, observe how completely unrhythmic, coarse-textured, fragmented, even jerky the following poem is: TOWN MEETING, by John Hay:

The meeting's in order. What's coming? What's to come?
The health officer says death. The carpenter
Says everything is shipshape. The minister
Says God — we try to say it too, like that.
But a frog croaks in our throats. Then nobody speaks.
For weeks. Isn't there something we mean to say?
Is the coming never to be come to? Speak!
Mr. Moderator, don't hold him down — the spark,
The star, the old, love-flinted animal.
Don't stop him saying what we knew before we came.

Yet both these types of poems, the definitely cadenced and strictly-rhyming, the broken, blunt, and more-nearly-conversational, are eminently modern, for both comment on our everyday contemporary world — more convincingly because of expert use or omission of like sound and regular beat.

• 4 •

Form

WHEN THE VARIOUS ELEMENTS of poetry we have already described are brought together in a rational manner, when there is order and method imposed upon or inherent in the material of the poet, we have form.

For the purposes of this discussion I have divided contemporary form into two categories, the *tonal* and the *lineal*. Let us begin with the latter, which is the more familiar. And by "lineal" I mean simply the form where the line, metrical arrangement, or rhyme is the predominant consideration.

Lineal Emphasis

As we all know, the rhyme schemes of earlier periods were more rigid; the reader bumped into similar sound at the end of a line like an engine hitting the block on a roundhouse turntable. But the modern poet attempts first of all to avoid the obvious and outworn; he may use the standard metrical arrangement of past times, but he wishes to be as casual and unrestricted, and often as camouflaged, as possible. Often he hopes to achieve the mood of the conversationalist or the man-on-the-street, in direct contrast to the exalted manner of the Victorian.

For example, let us see what Merrill Moore does with his verse: MRS. BRODERICK WAS A VERY UNUSUAL WOMAN —

But she was different from what most people thought.
They called her a hard woman, sinister,
But she was neither sinister nor hard;
That was a grotesque reputation nearly
Forgotten now by those who crossed her yard.

Actually she was extremely sympathetic.
Once when two Italian laborers were correcting
A leak in her cesspool she had a pitcher of lemonade
Sent out from her kitchen. They were not expecting
Such thoughtfulness; their gratitude was pathetic.

And another time she got up in the middle of the night
To pour ice water over some lobsters that
Were waiting in a sack to be boiled (alive) the next day;
She was a very unusual woman that way.

Here, the rhythms are ruled by a colloquial or off-beat style, and though the syntax is normal, its spread and temper are more like prose than the established notions of poetry. Also, the rhymes, "hard" "yard," "day" "way" are buried in half rhymes, slant rhythms, feminine endings, all of which give the feel of the natural and ironic disorder of the common-place. The words "sympathetic" and "correcting" pick up only a shade of like sound — but enough to give a muted effect. There is an evasiveness here, but it is the evasiveness of form that fits the divisiveness of our world. It gives a feeling of irregularity, spontaneity, and conversational ease. Even the title is made part of the poem. The strict rhymes are expendable — except at the end, where, appropriately enough, the emphatic "day"-"way" tends to bind together the paradox of the lady's life.

But there is another and different kind of casualness — an impromptu rebellion wherein the rhymes are more definite (though still not end-stopped and over-exact) but the chief effect is gained through the combined jolt of diction, imagery, and variation of metre. The technique here is to come a little closer to the conventional line-end rhymings while at the same time spicing them up by combining odd twists of word and thought with explosive metrical shifts. For example, note Felix Stefanile's VILLAGE ON MY BACK:

> Beneath the curve of hurried suns
> in their hot rain's track,
> I settled with my pain at once
> like a village on my back.
>
> My words, I strung them out like tents
> with banners full of my news,
> and my skin went around me like a fence,
> and I walked with a squeak in my shoes.
>
> Now as I grew the land I saw
> I named my charming south.
> My breath came merry and full of oh!
> but the winter pressed on my mouth:
>
> and like a fish I dove from sight
> beneath the eyes' lakes. Cleft
> I was, by a bump in the night.
> Ah the blood's a river full of craft.

In the last stanza "cleft" and "craft" are just enough off-beat to give shock; but more significant, the word "bump" is a jolt of the vernacular that disrupts flow and unity — and for that very reason assists the whole. Surely, "cleft" which is romantically acceptable, is a far cry from "bump," and this expertly reinforces the contrasts of the total theme. And the last line, "Ah the blood's a river full of craft," is a sharp deviation in metre, intentionally matter-of-fact or clumsy, to help carry the mood of intimacy with every-man. And all in all, these mutations have their impact *lineally* upon the form of the poem: one might say that the complete contour, the emotional shape and full lineal body, *catch up* with the reader during the last stanza.

Modern poetry employs more indirection in rhyming (and "indirection" identifies modern poetry in general better than any one word I know). Poets formerly attempted to *state* something, so that the idea might be conveyed directly to the reader; the current poet yearns, out of subconscious and borderland regions, to be born and give birth alike at one and the same moment of poetic being. Today, in keeping with this indirection, assonance, consonance, and partial rhymes of all types take the place of the old regular rhymes and melodic effects. Archibald MacLeish wrote all of his *Conquistador* with line-end assonance taking the place of rhyme. The world of chiaroscuros, elusives in form and meaning, paradoxes, and diagonals, is somehow more nearly the world of inward, poetic reality.

Today, there are all manner of shorthands and telescopings and scramblings of the recognizable. In Celia Dimmette's THE LAMB we read:

> In the storm, you came —
> Small one, the near

Muzzle, soft ear.
Wavering lamb.

We bring you from
The cold and stark
Stable of dark
Into our room,

Cry audible.
Newly you wake;
Stranger we stroke,
Be warm, grow wool.

Consider that sudden break, "Cry audible." The full, normal representation would demand "crying audibly," or "your cries audible." But the break-off and telescoping have two effects: First, if the writer simply means "your cries audible," it says it in such intense form that the intensity of the emotion is increased. But there is another gain: the reader can also take that "cry audible" to be the hortatory mood, a command, an entreaty suddenly made by himself, the reader, in an access of sympathy. This ambivalence actually enriches the reaction, for the heart and mind can encompass both experiences at once: the literal idea of the lamb's being brought into the room and "crying audibly," and the sense of his own heart, the reader's, exclaiming to the lamb: "O lamb, cry out, audibly, so that we may know you live and welcome your new-found life!" Thus reader-participation is increased; the violating of syntax, the short-cut compression have enhanced the beauty of the whole poem.

In addition to this kind of streamlining, parts of speech now take on new startling roles. The verb may become the noun, the noun the verb. For instance, note Alex Jackinson's poem, TELEVISION:

A dial twists;
centuries of invention spin back and forth
in a kaleidograph of miracles, no less fabulous
than water turned to wine
or Moses splitting the Red Sea,
hour after hour the parade
from cave to grandeur
from heights to sponsored scream.

This boxed triumph over epochs
could be redwood
majestic enough to touch stars;
in the packaged protoplasm of Sell
it becomes a greenhouse shrub
carefully cultivated, pruned and nurtured
to sprout magnificent blossoms
                                    of soap.

The word "Sell" functions as a noun.

And in the last stanza of THE SURGEON, by John Barron
Mays, we read:

Some day another's hands must close his eyes
And priest him unto death; till then he works
And trusts that someone other works through him
Close as a shadow to his healing hand.

The word "priest" acts very efficiently as a verb.

And in like manner we may have an adjective performing
as a verb or noun, a pronoun as an adverb.

The reason for this, of course, is that the modern poet is
concerned primarily with getting the idea across by means of
whatever words are most recognizable, in the form most
economical and easy to take. It may seem lax; but it does aid

compression and effect. Surely "And priest him unto death" is more convincing than "And like a priest reconcile him unto death" or "draw him unto death." In the syntax of modern poetry there are many gaps, there is much short-cutting.

What else would one expect in a world where we read, as we flash by: Go School Slow? Our minds have long since accepted it as a label, an automatic symbol, an ideogram which creates the reflex: "Go Slow: You're Coming To a School" — unarticulated in the mind, and therefore needing no coherent language to convey it. Or a big sign I saw over a new restaurant: Dinner Air Conditioned.

No effort was made to differentiate the parts of the idea by size or punctuation; the words were just strung together. But the jazzed and fragmented minds of passing citizens, accustomed to such hieroglyphs, readily substituted the idea of the inside atmosphere of the total restaurant for the idea of food on a plate, and caught the bare, fleeting intention of the words in their haste, which was all they cared about. Accuracy, reflection, nuance of meaning in such a world are admittedly difficult; but this kind of impressionism in advertising, these gesturings and snatches of sound indicate a reality of daily mood and reflex which in the interest of fidelity must be carried over into an impressionism, a compactness of poetry.

Difficult though subtlety may seem to be in a society so high-strung, nevertheless, subtlety is the very essence of modern poetry, and this includes its form and technique. By the use of nuance the modernist contributes to the relativity and individuality of fact; and the metre and syntax, the technique and form fluctuate correspondingly.

At one extreme, we have the tight, exact rhyme scheme of Theodore Roethke's The Sloth:

65

In moving-slow he has no Peer.
You ask him something in his ear;
He thinks about it for a Year;

And then, before he says a Word
There, upside down (unlike a Bird)
He will assume that you have Heard —

A most Ex-as-per-at-ing Lug.
But should you call his manner Smug,
He'll sigh and give his Branch a Hug;

Then off again to Sleep he goes,
Still swaying gently by his Toes,
And you must know he knows he knows.

At the other extreme, the long, rolling, uninhibited line of
Robinson Jeffers' THE DEER LAY DOWN THEIR BONES:

I followed the narrow cliffside trail, halfway up the
　　mountain
Above the deep river-canyon. There was a little
　　cataract crossed the path, flinging itself
Over tree-roots and rock, shaking the jewelled fern-
　　fronds, bright bubbling water
Pure from the mountain, but a bad smell came up.
　　Wondering at it I clambered down the steep
　　stream
Some forty feet, and found in the midst of bush-oak
　　and laurel
Hung like a bird's nest on the precipice brink a small
　　hidden clearing,
Grass and a shallow pool. But all about there were
　　bones lying in the grass, clean bones and
　　stinking ones,

Antlers and bones: I understood that the place was
    a refuge for wounded deer; there are so many
Hurt ones escape the hunter and limp away to lie
    hidden; here they have water for the awful
    thirst
And peace to die in; dense green laurel and grim
    cliff
Make sanctuary, and a sweet wind blows upward
    from the deep gorge.
    — I wish my bones were with theirs.

And, in between, lines from BUICK, by Karl Shapiro, where
regularity of metre gives form, but rhyme is lacking:

Flouncing your skirts, you blueness of joy, you
    flirt of politeness,
You leap, you intelligence, essence of wheelness
    with silvery nose,
And your platinum clocks of excitement stir like
    the hairs of a fern.

The modern poet no longer makes a fetish of *pattern* as
his predecessor did. *It need not be exact;* formalized arrangement can be broken. When he reveals most ardently the
personal psyche, he cuts adrift from the past. Freedom to be
the self creates its own form, out of the tilt of strange diction,
rebel idiom, explosive sound and rhythm — the changing
vistas of his own inward consciousness. As Robert Francis
put it so eloquently, in describing a flight of birds: "Freedom
that flows in form, and still is free."

Tonal Emphasis

Up to this point our discussion of form has been centered
upon the lineal: that is, the body of the poem in the metrical

round, its shape and more palpable design; but what of that other emphasis, the *tonal,* which deals with effluvium, aura, intangible essence? Often this in itself gives the pattern and unity; the totality is not one of visual range, but of consistent sound stress and fillip. The mood enters the heart through the play upon the senses and through half-felt import, rather than the *lineally and metrically controlled.*

The meaning and feel of the poem become real through its *cumulative* tonal-sensuous treatment, rather than through any literalness of statement or dependence upon exterior manner. This kind of verse works from the inside out, builds up effect, steals up to overtake the reader.

Much of modern verse still pays tribute to the romantic mood, a legitimate fealty, especially if it breaks away from the strict line-and-rhyme patterns of the nineteenth century, whose too-mechanical regularities have become flat and trite. When they are sloughed off, the modern poem, even though the temper may be of the long-established, seems more like a distinctly new and contemporary thing.

The romantically tonal poem in the modern sphere, then, would be a logical beginning point for our fresh tack: for example, Isabella Gardner's GIMBOLING:

Nimble as dolphins to
dive leap and gimble, sleep, supple
as ripples to slip around each other to
wander and fondle on under and into
the seeking and coupling and swarming of water
compliant as sea-plants to bend with the tide
unfolding and folding to frond and to flower
a winding and twining to melt and to merge
to rock upon billowing founder in surf
and a fathom's down drowning before the sweet waking
the floating ashore into sleep and to morning.

It is easy to see at once that the sound of the words renders beautifully the sense, the import, the intent of the poem. One might call it an extended play in onomatopoeia. A beauty, a sensuous, sinuous liveliness emerges with the sound; in "sleek, supple / as ripples to slip around each other to / wander and fondle on under and into / the seeking and coupling and swarming of water" the hushing, limpid movement is felt not as idea but as experience, as *being* and *identification* on the part of the reader. And this is largely because there is no pointing out, no explanation-through-technique; nothing of the explicit intrudes. The form is gained through the unity of tone. No rhyme occurs; line-length matters little; and though lines like "unfolding and folding to frond and to flower" have a regular cadence, they are lost in total emanation, do not impinge upon us lineally to any marked degree. (Note, by the way, in keeping with former discussion, how the word "founder," a verb, is used as a noun.)

At the other extreme of mood — non-romantic, harsh, and dissonant, but thoroughly modern — we have such a poem as Jed Garrick's ANSWER IN BRIGHT GREEN:

into their gray house I will not go
and when their lemon lips find me in the market-place
I shall laugh panurge at them
and when they polyp-shake my hand I shall prick them
with solomon and minarets . . . .
and when they beam me holy in the street
my easter island face will rock against their eyes
and I will not go into their gray houses.

and when they say me no in the bright morning
I shall give them breughel yes and falstaff
while they sip pekoe I shall pour rich burgundy
on the roots of a scarlet rose

and when they tell me sunday and stewed beef
my answer will be asteroids and nectar
and with two fingers I shall draw a sign in air
to exorcise the no they say on a bright morning.

Here the words fall into two categories: Those of the rebel
who is taunting the respectable citizenry: "panurge," "prick,"
"rock," "breughel yes," "falstaff," "pour"; and, on the other
hand, the attributes of staid propriety: "gray," "lemon lips,"
"beam me holy," "sip pekoe," "sunday and stewed beef."

(And, by the way, again in keeping with our earlier reference to shorthand in modern verse, note how succinctly he says
"beam at me to try to make me holy," or "beam at me in their
holy manner" — it becomes a mere "beam me holy." And, instead of a full statement, "my face, symbol of my private self,
which, like an island, has its own concepts of joy and resurrec-
tion, rocks against them defiantly," he gives us the terse and
vivid "my easter island face will rock against their eyes,"
leaving us to meet the challenge and discover for ourselves,
reap the adventure of arranging, filling in meaning with the
flesh of our own emotion.)

We have two groupings of words; but is there a decided
difference in tonal quality between them? No, the categories
are both unpleasant, harsh, realistic rather than romantic, and
even *gauche*. For example, "sunday and stewed beef," though
it describes religious zealots, is anything but idealistic in mode;
rather, it plows up further soil of sarcasm and rocky satire
which was first laid open by "lemon lips," "polyp-shake" and
other words of category number one. And where, offhand,
"with solomon and minarets" might seem to be a verging on
the romantic, if we re-examine our reaction at that point, we
shall find that the very idea of pricking the people with a Solomon is so radical that it adds to the droll and satirical humor
of the whole texture.

Moving on, there are poems which seek to combine the romantic tonal quality with modern cohesion. The palpable form — ready outline of line and metre — is still de-emphasized; but unity is sought stealthily — by a definite pattern of sound or technical arrangement. We'll take the poem MOWING THE LAWN from my own work:

Across the sheen of whirl and daisies
glazing the cordial flurr of sun,
spun in lower dark of worm,

birds around, branches dancing,
lance of steel in daisies shorn;
turned to upper curve of bird wing —
storm of gold and green vortex;
reflex: hurry, love, and humming.

Metal, metal, tender in cutting,
whetting the edge of all men's summers;
wonder of Junes, the hot spore
stored at the root; the sticking soil.

Grass, grass, green as my heart-beat
fleet with the hurry of Jesus' pain;
rain of his pleasure, cut grass, leaping,
deep as his freshness along men's veins —

green as his vortex of pity cut,
shut from the earth of answering love.
Give, earth; teach; rejoin my brain
to his thought, his gold daisy clash

brash as sun and humus scent,
blended of spore and love and heat,
sweet-clicking, low, and metal bright

as the tight nails I rip free
from his tree of death, his builder hands,
glad that the concept of crucifix
is myth; there is only his joyous striding.

The tone here is one of passionate reverence, and a *revelling in* that mood — obviously an attitude employed often in the sentimental poetry of the past. But there is much departure from established norms in the dart and shock of idea (for example, tying in machinery with mercy and divine love); and the form has been reinforced with two techniques which I call "reverse rhyme" and "interlocking rhyme."

Historically, the emphasis in poetry has been on sound at the end of the line. But there are two strong positions in any unit of thought: beginning and ending. Why not strengthen the start of the line too? The poem therefore attempts "reverse rhyme" — couplet or alternate rhymes (full, slant, half, or assonant) coming somewhere in the *first foot*. And further to encourage this blending and balance, this underscoring at two positions rather than one, the "interlocking rhyme" is introduced, in which the last word of a line rhymes (full, slant, half, or assonant) with *some part of the first foot of the next.*

In the first stanza "daisies" at the end of the first line, ties in slantwise with "glazing" at the beginning of the next. Here it is the *first* syllable of the first foot of the line which rhymes with the last word of the previous line; but in the next to last stanza "bright" has its sound picked up in the *third* syllable of the fourth line by "tight." Or the tie-in may be with the second syllable of that first foot of the line. In like manner, the reverse rhyme may drift leisurely in and out; in stanza three, "metal" (line one) is picked up by "whetting" (line two).

And finally, let us consider Richard Eberhart's lyric poem,
GO TO THE SHINE THAT'S ON A TREE:

> Go to the shine that's on a tree
> When dawn has laved with liquid light
> With luminous light the nighted tree
> And take that glory without fright.
>
> Go to the song that's in a bird
> When he has seen the glistening tree,
> That glorious tree the bird has heard
> Give praise for its felicity.
>
> Then go to the earth and touch it keen,
> Be tree and bird, be wide aware
> Be wild aware of light unseen,
> And unheard song along the air.

The poem is housed in an outwardly traditional arrangement of metre, sound, and cadence; the tone is romantic. But note how regularity of form conceals an inner device — a "pick up" effect — of repetition and dilation: "liquid light/luminous light;" "glistening tree/glorious tree;" "wide aware/wild aware." A modern technique, which increases tension, momentum, like the passing of another car on the open road — the quick thrust of the accelerator, the easing back, the clear road again. And through this acceleration, this hidden explosiveness, comes a cohesion that is distinctly fresh and contemporary.

In this and many similar attempts by a wide range of poets, modern verse hopes to *permit* form to become a *oneness,* to achieve *identity with* meaning and tone, as the sky permits color-through-light not only to express but to *become* itself — rather than to impose form upon material like the stamping of an image upon a coin.

• 5 •
Idea

WE HAVE DEALT with some of the basic characteristics that set off the modern poem from its predecessors: the uses of imagery, word-selection, rhythm, form, and structure — all of them involving the vehicle of language, and the poet's skill and imagination in using it. But every poem also involves *idea* — the force by which it is animated, its very heart and substance. Without idea, whether intellectually or emotionally inspired, poetry would become merely a linguistic or aesthetic exercise (as some very nearly do).

By idea we don't mean necessarily the topic of the poem. The topic, the subject-matter, is the stuff with which the dummy is clothed; idea brings it to life. The choice of subject, like the poet's use of imagery, rhythm, form, and so forth, contributes to the idea, and thus to the total effect of the poem. In this chapter the various components we have discussed so far may come into consideration as they reinforce idea.

74

Throughout literary history it has been the efficacy of the idea (through the medium of the poet's skill) that has set off the strong, the enduring, the great poetry from the weak or mediocre. It is the truth of the poet's idea relative to the total human experience *and for his own age* that gives his work strength and value. For modern poetry this must be the criterion, as it has been in the past. But what, then, sets off the modern poem from its predecessors? How does it differ from the traditional with respect to idea?

To find the answer glance for a moment at our twentieth-century physical world, with its ethos and mores, and compare it with what we know of the world of 1850 or 1710, 1600 or 1490. As our planet has shrunk, our consciousness, our mental world has grown outward, and at an enormously accelerated pace in the last fifty or sixty years. The impact of scientific, technological, social, and psychological change upon all the arts has broadened their reach. It has brought with it unprecedented experimentation, individuality, diversity, and nonconformity.

True, nonconformity, fierce individuality, rebellion have been almost the traditional marks of the great poet — Wordsworth, Shelley, Whitman — but the manner of presentation then was more assimilable. Eloquence, elevation, skill in the manipulation of the familiar sentiments were often requisites for honor. There was a more universal response in the artist because of a greater uniformity of culture. In past generations, ideas acceptable in poetic expression were more homogeneous to the ethos and mores of the day. And so we may say that idea in modern poetry differs from the traditional in its expanded scope and range, in the limitless *kinds of ideas* upon which the modern poet may draw.

In range and in *depth*. This is not to say that modern

poetry has come up with human truths any more profound than those revealed by Shakespeare and others. But advances in the study of human psychology, the overthrow of ancient codes, and the freedom to explore openly what was formerly taboo, all allow the modern poet to probe further, to reach into the subconscious, to delve everywhere and interminably to unearth the particular, no matter how stinging or drab.

The idea, as expressed in contemporary poetry, also differs in its handling. Both traditional and modern may deal with the same concepts, the same age-old universal human truths, but it is their interpretation that sets them apart. The present-day poet is faced by a larger, far more complex, unstable world, and if his work is sometimes sordid, blunt, fragmented, staccato, he is only true to the nature of his age. Where the poet of past times was more declarative, today's poet handles his ideas more subtly and indirectly.

But his chief opportunity, his glory, is still the fact that he can pioneer in ideas — ideas that mold the old truth to the new or illuminate a fresh and terrifying awareness for mankind, ideas that titillate and shock, and bewilder and satirize and desecrate. It is paradoxical that with greater freedom of expression today, with means of communication undreamed-of fifty years ago, so much of the creative output in every sector of our culture seems ever more bland, pallid and homogenized; all the more reason, therefore, that the poet can be — must be — the iconoclast.

One of the most virulent myths the modern poet must cope with is the still popular belief that poetry should deal only with certain sentiments, honeybee and toilet-water varieties. But it is poetry's virtue, its strength, that it can invade every province. The essential articulation of what we are, it must breathe the individuality of life.

While contemporary poetry is faced with popular misconception, it is — as we have mentioned — vulnerable to the criticism that it has lost touch with today's readership, that it tends to be obscure and academic. Why do so many readers avoid modern poetry? We can blame this neglect on the development of mass media, easy-to-acquire entertainment, the popularity of the novel, but too many talented modern poets dissipate their force and authority in the flattering little world of the devoted coterie. They are susceptible to preoccupation with newness for its own sake; self-conscious cleverness is often abetted by today's higher criticism, which tends to think too much about the *way* a thing is said, rather that *what* is being said. Technique obviates content; vitality is lost. It has been said that this generation fears emotion and its expression, is afraid of commitment. But it is through commitment that ideas assume their force and strength — through commitment that the poet can live up to the axiom that he is the "unacknowledged legislator of the world."

Obviously we cannot begin to encompass the whole range of idea in modern poetic expression, but let us consider how some of these ideas are handled.

Many progressive poets today offer their themes with a degree of intellectualism, dignity, and declarative directness characteristic of the traditional. We'll begin with RALPH WALDO EMERSON RECEIVES A VISIT FROM A SANE MAN AND REJECTS HIM, by James Schevill:

> By way of authority he knocks
> On my door as if there were no locks.
> Perhaps he is a joker of my brain
> This sane man unwet in the rain.
> Anonymous as an apple and decreed
> To conformity in word and deed,

His mind is straight and never leaning
Pressured only in the single meaning.
He knocks at me as the punctual image
Who drives the Industrial Age.
How shallow is our doctrine of beauty!
We have fled the perceptive eye and
Drained the dependence of form on soul.
The sane man has become our goal.
It is hard to reject him. He comes
In clothes and language of common homes
But I do reject him. I cast
Him to the gaffing privateer that is the past,
For I believe in one soul related to the world.
We see this world piece by piece, not hurled
From cautious suns to shine in goods
Which cage our spirit's claws with hawking hoods.
Only the fixing of soul's pieces together
Shall discover the white-bait weather.
As sea and earth are one with sky
So mind and heart must unite in the eye,
The lost voice be freed from the terror
Of isolation and the sane man's error
Soar into the jagged soul under
The nailed cross and sing in wonder.

The ideas here might well be those of a man in Tennyson's time. But there are elements outside the idea that identify it as a product of the avant-garde — the vernacular "joker of my brain," the tougher and more elusive quality of the figures of speech — "shall discover the white-bait weather" — (whereas the effects in older verse were more immediately perceptible) and the roughness, almost jerkiness of meaning, sound, organization here, to keep the sense closer to the prosaic, the actuality of life.

Nevertheless, this poem could well be characterized in its

general thought-approach and tone as being akin to the idea-verse of earlier periods — explicit, dignified, discursive, with prose normalcy in sequence and syntax. For example, "As sea and earth are one with sky / So mind and heart must unite in the eye / And the lost voice be freed from the terror / Of isolation . . ." might well be a quote from Frost or Masefield.

Or there is the modern idea which superficially may resemble the work of former times because of its recognizable *romantic* sentiment. Here is George P. Elliott's THE GIFT:

> I dreamed I held you in my arms
> bowered in greenest secrecy,
> Wisdom fell off like clothes among the hours,
> And owl sang love all night
> In his mildest key.
>
> My arms knew who it was they held
> But not whose wild and special stir.
> How could they know, for all the lapping light,
> You were not only who
> You seemed to be?
>
> Naked in the green night I lay
> And owl sang from his highest bough.
> Some goddess in your flesh gave gift of power,
> Who, I shall never know,
> Nor who you are.

And yet, here too there is an abruptness of manner, a *shift* and range and *breaking off* in rhythm or diction, an undertone of the intransigent and acrid that sets it in the midst of new trends. For example: "I dreamed I held you in my arms / bowered in greenest secrecy. / Wisdom fell off like clothes among the hours, / [note especially] And owl sang love all night / In his mildest key." But it does deal with idea essentially as its forerunners did: it uses the more romantic equipage: the owl, the "green night," the goddess, the "lapping light," the "highest bough."

There is, however, the modern poem which, at the level of idea, cannot be mistaken for any older relation. Note, for instance, To a Bird Outside the Window, by the same George Elliott:

> Little bird, I do not know
> What you are called or why you sing;
> I do not know, when winter comes,
> What you will fear or where you'll go.
>
> I rarely see the world you're in
> And ill at ease I see you now;
> For you like money call to mind
> A world where I have never been.

This poem breaks wide open in the second line from the end: "For you like money call to mind / A world where I have never been."

How startling that word "money"! The exaltation and propriety, the romantic gentleness of the preceding might well belong to the nineteenth century — and then the crassness of "money" explodes the whole poem sky-high. Of course, there is that lurking, half-wistful humor in the final announcement; but its action upon us is a delayed one; the immediate and overwhelming effect is the incongruity of cold, bald economic consideration in juxtaposition to the airy and lambent thoughts preceding; it is the contrast *idea* which ignites the experience for us and hurls us out from the center. Who, in

80

a more conventional realm of poetry, would think of comparing a dear, sweet little bird, affectionately introduced, to cold cash?

This is a common device of the new poet: to create effect by shock in idea (as well as in other things); to throw different weights and values into ironic contrast by deft use of *juxtaposition*. This kind of rugged treatment was not accorded the reader of more tender eras. Today, like the celluloid toy on a lead base that rocks back to upright when smacked down to the floor, the reader must become accustomed to violent abuse. But how much more exciting the experience of poetry can become when we are thus handled: whereas irritation can inflame, the zephyr stultifies; the unexpected reveals, but the long-known deludes.

In the most truly modern poem, simple, unadorned vitality of thought can thrive — the idea emerging out of the heat-cloud of present-day language and custom as cleanly as a jet out of a thunderhead. As, for example, in Kenneth Beaudoin's PASTORAL POEM:

> upon a beach towel
> (dyes by Dupont)
> beneath a parasol
> (sears and roebuck 2.98)
> upon a cocacola bottle
> picnic napkin paper cup
> cigarette butt strewn beach
> the mother nurses child
> pulling the primordic sacrament
> into the present
> from the earth ancient past
> as easily
> as buttons switch on lights,
> motors move wheels.

Here is one idea, one comparison of images on which our attention is focused by the highly effective means — because they are all contemporaneous and unitary — of rhythm, imagery, succinctness, and casual sophistication.

The modernist triumphs because he can reveal or celebrate things precisely as they are, in the private limbo and the public arena, and he need bring no dogma or prejudgment to his art. He is emancipated; like a child he wallows in the *being* of things for their own sake. He can be tumultuous and brutal with the concreteness of experience, in the naked display of his perceptive powers; he can be insurgent beyond all boundaries, an advocate of his own existentialism. Far more than his forerunners, he can shake us with revolt against fact by the sheer frontal weight of fact-presentation — as in these lines from THE DEATH OF A BALL TURRET GUNNER by Randall Jarrell:

From my mother's sleep I fell into the State,
And I hunched in its belly till my wet fur froze.
Six miles from earth, loosed from its dream of life,
I woke to black flak and the nightmare fighters.
When I died they washed me out of the turret with a hose.

As we have noted, idea is fundamental to the whole bent and fortune of a poetic work. A reader wants to know what the idea-intention of the work is, what it adds up to as meaning-relative-to-me. In poetry, as in the other arts, whether consciously or not, we look for nourishment as well as sensuous titillation. Philosophic value has a place — in substance, implication, or delayed reflex. And every legitimate means, imagery and diction, rhythm and sound, can contribute to that effect.

82

What happens when we have finished with a poem? If the idea-element has been important to the author, and at the same time has been harmonious with truth, it will carry conviction. Whether superficial or weighty, the idea-residue — or what remains after our emotional reaction has subsided — will persist in our consciousness as one of the significant facets of the work. When a poem is screened by later generations, the depth and power of the idea presented help determine its authority and length of life. True, the casual pieces, with their fresh realizations of an old experience at the purely sensuous level, or the new non-intellectual, objective experiencing of the world about us, have some validity. But are they anything more than mere decoration?

Much as the modernist may contribute to the advancement of his art through deviation and new esthetics, are there not deeps that must be sounded, if poetry is to be more than craft? Is there not a range of value in the *ideas* of poetry as well as in the *ways* they are expressed?

In spite of the variety of possible fluctuations, there are continuities of principle with which most of us have affinity, and, regardless of our personal inadequacies, we continue to respond to them. That response, to a large extent, is the final arbiter.

One of the ultimate judgments of art, as of all things, is still non-creedal, intuitive morality. The poem might not explicitly say one word of good, evil, or virtue, but the moral *intent* of the author is known, and scaled and fixed accordingly in the memory of the reader. And no matter how much the poet may pretend or expostulate, his moral conclusions about the eternal issues radiate from every line. By ideas, essentially, he justifies his existence (though he must not set out deliberately to do so). Whatever code sustains him delivers him into the spiritual hands of men, and by that spirit of common wisdom, more than by passing esthetic standards, will he be cherished or rejected, heeded or ignored.

Man's fulfillment in the world of art depends upon the establishment of rapport between his social psyche and that of the artist — in the areas of reality they have both arrived at through growth. The awareness they have attained *in common* allows response to any particular poetic expression.

In spite of the multitude of tight, singular poems that issue today, there are many writers who venture out onto the wider and more virile scene. But the mere fact that they tap social reality does not automatically mean they produce the best poetry; much of what they do is far from virile, and is anything but an integration of the best elements of the art.

Let us look at a few examples which work with ideas, as oriented to the social psyche, and see how they succeed or fail. CALLING ALL GRANDCHILDREN, by Lilith Lorraine:

Never believe what they say who must pass their world to
    your keeping,
The world that they turned from peace while the shadow of
    fear was creeping.
Over the change-born dream that no blood-dipped slogan
    could smother,
Over the beautiful land that took the world for its brother.
Never believe what they say who barter their young like
    chattels,
Less than the tiger and wolf who fight their own perilous
    battles,
Look at their outthrust tongues and their horrible rat-gray
    faces,
Leering from every screen and defiling the holiest places.
Look deep in their greed-slitted eyes, at their cold lips thick
    with their lying,

Mouthing the great numbers of youth that is marked for the
    dying —
Give them no word of quarter, for all space is yours for the
    winning.
For you are the Golden Races, foretold from the world's
    beginning.

Can we say this poem is successful? Why not? It is weak-
ened, to a great extent by clichés; the rhythm is too pronounced, like a popular tune; the ideas are too *ideological;*
the social lends itself too readily to the facile and didactic.
(The author has done much fine work, and this example is
chosen only to illustrate a point.) We live in a community
atmosphere saturated with trite aphorism, sermonizing, codi-
fied behavior. All this, as much as we may fight it, too often
penetrates the manner and content of our poetry. Abstract
ideas of good and evil are always harder to handle in a fresh
way: they have been so formalized for mass consumption by
the total culture that the most original invention picks up some
of the toxic dust.

Let us look now at another approach to social reality. Here
is Lawrence Ferlinghetti's No. 3 in A CONEY ISLAND OF THE
MIND:

The poet's eye obscenely seeing
sees the surface of the round world
    with its drunk rooftops
    and wooden oiseaux on clotheslines
    and its clay males and females
    with hot legs and rosebud breasts
    in rollaway beds
and its trees full of mysteries
and its Sunday parks and speechless statues
and its America
    with its ghost towns and empty Ellis Islands

and its surrealist landscape of
                    mindless prairies
                    supermarket suburbs
                    steamheated cemeteries
                    cinerama holy days
                    and protesting cathedrals
a kissproof world of plastic toiletseats tampax and taxis
        drugged store cowboys and las vegas virgins
        disowned indians and cinemad matrons
        unroman senators and conscientious non-objectors
'and all the other fatal shorn-up fragments
of the immigrant's dream come too true
        and mislaid
                    among the sunbathers

Why is this poem more effective? For one thing, by drama-
tizing his experience in the concrete, the living palpable act,
in the fresh non-didactic idea, the poet allows his audience
to discover much of the implication, moral or otherwise. He
does not preach or overstate; there is no pretentiousness, no
bombast or soap-boxing. The moral *intent* is there, but it is
more implicit than explicit.

And even when the poem is more an overt statement, an
explicit moral exhortation, it can be done with economy,
freshness, and dramatic zest. Observe Kenneth Patchen's O
FIERY RIVER:

> O fiery river
> Flow out over the land.
> Men have destroyed the roads of wonder,
> And their cities squat like black toads
> In the orchards of life.
> Nothing is clean, or real, or as a girl,
> Naked to love, or to be a man with.
> The arts of this American land

Stink in the air of mountains;
What has made these men sick rats
That they find out every cheap hole?

How can these squeak of greatness?
Push your drugstore-culture into the sewer
With the rest of your creation.
The bell wasn't meant to toll for you.
Keep your filthy little hands off it.

O fiery river
Spread over this American land.
Drown out the falsity, the smug contempt
For what does not pay . . .
What would you pay Christ to die again?

Just as there is a range, then, in the value of poetry, according to its idea-content, so there is a range in the success of the socially oriented poetry, according to the technical efficiency of the poet. And perhaps the most distinctive technique of the modernist, as we have indicated earlier, is his use of *indirection*. And nowhere is this more important than in the handling of verse of the social psyche, those deep areas which, in the broad public, are replete with dogma, triteness, banality. The poet when bearing the great verities must often come upon his audience unobtrusively.

One poem, quoted earlier, dealt with two contrasting themes rooted in the social psyche of every one of us: war and world brotherhood. Let us see how different modern poets handle one of these subjects, then both together. First, the more direct and obvious attack upon the conditions that breed and issue from war: one by George Penner, called PRESCRIPTION FOR FAINT HEARTS:

Are you pale, tired, always afraid?
Do you feel distress when eating
Your own fears?
Or when others are not eating?
Have you tried yogurt, yogi, blackstrap
And blaming all blacks
And reds?
Does the price of coffee keep you awake
And the price of war?

Then keep following their simple directions:
Vitamin A wise man asks no questions.
Vitamin B careful we are watching.
Vitamin C no evil.
Vitamin Despair is the only answer.
Take daily until
Dead.

And the other, by James Schevill, CONFIDENTIAL DATA ON
THE LOYALTY INVESTIGATION OF HERBERT ASHENFOOT:

Until the birth of my thirtieth birthday
I walked in the wide harbor of illusion,
Wind and war of parents over my silent head
While the curse of identity tinkled
At my window like the Good Humor salesman.
Around me the black armies like bats
Lay darkly in their caves of caution
And for security I joined the Civil Service.
Rating P-3, almost a pristine pursuit plane,
I roared from basket in to basket out
And all my days were clocked and carefree.
At the dawn of thirty my reform began.
My loyalty was cleaned and prodded
And my dreams divorced from all emergencies.

Propped at a desk with aspirin I typed
In the tears of my time like a hermit crab.

It can be observed here that both Penner and Schevill couch their indignation in the *indirection* of sarcasm and irony — not too quiet, perhaps, but persuasive.

From irony we move on to paradox, often the most indirect and subtle means of fusing the social psyches of artist and audience — and the most effective. Here is Winfield Townley Scott's THE U. S. SAILOR AND THE JAPANESE SKULL:

Bald-bare, bone-bare, and ivory yellow: skull
Carried by a thus two-headed U. S. sailor
Who got it from a Japanese soldier killed
At Guadalcanal in the ever-present war: our

Bluejacket, I mean, aged 20, in August strolled
Among the little bodies on the sand and hunted
Souvenirs: teeth, tags, diaries, boots; but bolder still
Hacked off this head and under a leopard tree skinned it:

Peeled with a lifting knife the jaws and cheeks, bared
The nose, ripped off the black-haired scalp and gutted
The dead eyes to these thoughtful hollows: a scarred
But bloodless job, unless it be said brains bleed.

Then, his ship underway, dragged this aft in a net
Many days and nights — the cold bone tumbling
Beneath the foaming wake, weed-worn and salt-cut
Rolling safe among fish and washed with Pacific;

Till on a warm and level-keeled day hauled in
Held to the sun and the sailor, back to a gun-rest,
Scrubbed the cured skull with lye, perfecting this:
Not foreign as he saw it first: death's familiar cast.

Bodiless, fleshless, nameless, it and the sun
Offend each other in strange fascination
As though one of the two were mocked; but nothing is in
This head, or it fills with what another imagines

As: here were love and hate and the will to deal
Death or kneel before it, death emperor,
Recorded orders without reasons, bomb-blast, still
A child's morning, remembered moonlight on Fujiyama:

All scoured out now by the keeper of this skull
Made elemental, historic, parentless by our
Sailor boy who thinks of home, voyages laden, will
Not say, "Alas! I did not know him at all."

Here, out of an apparently detached and brooding treatment, the idea catches us with delayed reaction. All the better. The complete thought-impact, finally achieved, is that
the very things we are taught to hate and destroy in war
(symbolized by the skull) are those that teach us the similarity
of dreams, loyalties, loves in all men — brotherhood. Particularly well is this managed in the understatement at the end:
"who thinks of home, voyages laden, will / Not say, 'Alas! I
did not know him at all.' " Actually, he has come to know
him in the truest sense, and most completely.

How does the poet's social perception quicken our own?
We get the idea not at the level of the propagandist and the
politician — the explicit prose level — but through all the
hidden springs of tenuous emotion, the inner rooms and cor-
ridors of half-known, half-forgotten revelation. We become
re-acquainted with ourselves and the reality of all mortal
community by the lightest touch of the poet's fingers — grace
and strength more manifest in the tentative than in the
abrupt and demanding. We meet resistance in his lines, his

style; his meanings elude for a moment — but that is why, as with the lover who tantalizes, the consummation is all the more electric.

Often a poet may be deceptive: he may employ indirection, an elusive power to capture us, by a very direct and simple style, a mastery of the everyday, the poignantly familiar.

Consider FOLK SONG by William Pillin:

Dear to me is the song of my people
like a whispered lament
through my heart's clear channel.

In flutter of excited words it moves
like an echo's monument to silence,
like leaves blowing
                            into the nightwind.

On murder seeded plain it moves,
in raven haunted towns
through darkness of wings beating panic.
Wherever I go in the world
I hear the song of my people pleading
for one more day before terrors gleam
like red meteors of anger
and the music disappears
                            among frightened chimneys.

In a handful of wheat I find it,
in silver rustle
of slender aspens, in wave swept kindling,
the song of my people pleading
for one more day
before mist scatters swallows of light

> and the heart is a dead bird
> > endlessly falling.

What do we perceive here? Notice in the lines from the first stanza, "A whispered lament / through my heart's clear channel," how the poet evokes nostalgic affection and compassion. And then: "On murder seeded plain it moves, / in raven haunted towns / through darkness of wings beating panic." The concept of immortality, which has given us myth and legend and saint, infuses the poet with reverence for the transient. And that, we are aware, is what drives and informs him:

> . . . my people pleading
> for one more day before terrors gleam
> like red meteors of anger
> and the music disappears

Simple imagery and everyday diction reinforce the genuineness of emotion. "Among frightened chimneys." What could be more universally symbolic of the home, the most inward emotions and thoughts of humanity, than the chimney, from which the smoke of intimate hearth-fires rises?

Through universalizing and simplifying, through understatement, the poem acquires intensity. We see the particular words are direct, yet the over-all manner is tangential, elusive; Pillin evokes a great deal beyond the apparent. The total idea is reinforced. And in the final stanza:

> the song of my people pleading
> for one more day
> before mist scatters swallows of light
> and the heart is a dead bird
> > endlessly falling

Birds and light. What do we associate with them? Freedom. In this case, universal concepts of freedom from labor and oppression. And the final line, "endlessly falling"? Pillin gives us a revelation of cataclysm; he announces fatalistic truth, one of the strongest bonds in life or death, between us, between *folk*. The poem conveys a belief in people. Pillin despairs, but his sorrow is locked in mankind.

Poetic ideas can break open, challenge, violate, create controversy. One of the offices of higher poetry can be — and has been — to expose the sacrosanct. How does one modern poet do it? Consider three brief examples by Lawrence Lipton. First a challenge to the cult of Science-with-a-capital-S, INQUEST:

> Giordano Bruno chemically changed
> By thermal action; Jesus on the cross
> A rearrangement of the particles.
> The man of science with his final breath
> Defies the event: a thermodynamically
> Stable configuration known as death.

Or the TV-Radio gods of Advertising? Take these lines from FANFARE FOR A DELAYED EXIT:

> . . . .
> The perfect word, lowvoiced and sure,
> Timed with trembling prescience; spoken
> Without fear, and heard a world away —
> Now sold on measured scales of time
> As once they panned a profit from
> The brain-pan of a Watt or Faraday;
> Chain lightning to sell nostrums,
> Sex and sadism dished up between
> Slices of Denatured Bread;

By courtesy of beer and aspirin
Our lists of battle dead.

Or in WITH EINSTEIN'S FIDDLE the pretensions of the Science-Religion harmonizers in the pulpit:

Friends, when you nibble your nails
Be sure you swallow pieces
Lest the Liberal Clergy find them
And conjure with them.

They patched up Genesis with three hairs
From the beard of Darwin.
Who knows what they shall yet do
With Einstein's fiddle?

What are the elements which give these poems value? The very qualities which challenge and disturb. With Lipton, the idea predominates, clear, powerful, and present-day. We feel its impact, not by indirection, but by forthrightness, audacity. The poet seeks to call attention to the points of our psychological imbalance or hypocrisy. Those of tender sensibilities may quiver at such gall, but it is part and parcel of what made Whitman or Thoreau. In modern terms, Lipton achieves the age-old position of the poet as iconoclast who satirizes in order to shock us into awareness and growth.

But so far we have dwelt on ideas that encompass the humanitarian. What of the religious and mystical? No field of poetry has more pitfalls than this, none is more susceptible to banality, to sermonizing, to thinly disguised "moral lessons" for the elevation of the reader. In no area of recent popular verse is the Victorian residue more apparent. Such verse, well-meaning as it may be, most often fails because it is didactic, or because the subjects are presented in a flowery or sentimental manner. Lacking challenge and freshness, it fails to stir a response in us. Take for example these lines from a poem by James K. Williams:

Bliss can be yours. Will you now begin it?
Come nearer to God with every minute?
Then, pave with love each golden mile,
For Heaven waits in the Afterwhile!

Or these lines from DON'T MAKE THE ANGELS CRY, by Pat Harshbarger:

When I heard my child in prayer
I softly added, "Please take care."
For how do you tell a child so small
That before long, God will call?
Do you tell him there will be no pain;
There will always be sunshine, never rain?
That he can play on streets of gold,
The hand of the Lord will never scold? . . .

In contrast, how does the new poet interpret a religious subject? Let us begin with e. e. cummings, one of the pioneer modernists, and see how he deals with a conventional subject in an unconventional manner, in A MAN WHO HAD FALLEN AMONG THIEVES:

a man who had fallen among thieves
lay by the roadside on his back
dressed in fifteenthrate ideas
wearing a round jeer for a hat

fate per a somewhat more than less
emancipated evening

had in return for consciousness
endowed him with a changeless grin

whereon a dozen staunch and leal
citizens did graze at pause
then fired by hypercivic zeal
sought newer pastures or because

swaddled with a frozen brook
of pinkest vomit out of eyes
which noticed nobody he looked
as if he did not care to rise

one hand did nothing on the vest
its wideflung friend clenched weakly dirt
while the mute trouserfly confessed
a button solemnly inert

Brushing from whom the stiffened puke
i put him all into my arms
and staggered banged with terror through
a million billion trillion stars

Notice how he draws us to the godly and ecstatic samaritan.
The Good Samaritan, of course, was the off-beat guy, the non-
conformist who shamed the respectable. His act of mercy was
the prototype of all charity — to "do good to the least of these
my brethren" being a chief admonition of any faith — because
the needy one was dirty, wounded, difficult to handle, and
most of all, a member of a despised enemy society. It has been
said that in uplifting the weak, suffering, or broken, there is an
unmatched religious exaltation. The more abysmal, repulsive,
or heretic the sin or condition, the greater the rapture of as-
sistance. How does Cummings create in us this glory and

wonder, this closeness to God in the holy *deed,* the spontaneous act of self-humbling, fully-committed *love?* In absolutely unique, unconventional, completely modern terms and language. What says it better than these last three lines?

> i put him all into my arms
> and staggered banged with terror through
> a million billion trillion stars.

The "stars" are the very presence of God. There is a "terror" in being pulled thus into the heart of God's being by the supreme act man can perform; he is awed by a sort of religious vision and exhilaration; he himself is almost deified; and to feel such triumph and joy and blinding sweetness of revelation is frightening, to be so identical with God is to be overwhelmed, stunned. What religious experience could be more genuine, what moment more godly? The modern immediacy is reinforced through such words as *"banged* with terror"; the occult, extrahuman wonder and power are conveyed through the pile-up of sound: a *million, billion, trillion* stars." Through the crescendo of numbers a sense of the immensity of God's own affection for man is achieved.

Again, in modern poetry in which the religious idea is paramount, consider how the poet may probe beyond God-in-society, into the mystical, the relationship of man to all nature, all forces in the infinite universes. We'll take my attempt in TRAFFIC QUINCE:

> When you see the traffic light
> brighten with red, and reach
> the clear thorn of warning far,
> starring the city air, — then there,
> there is the quince bush within whose flare
> the tired driver plunges flesh:

the mesh of Christ, no less, the love
swung forth from wires and poles of grace.
No face of Jesus rose more clear
to bare the fault, to still the weary.
He cared for traveller whose eyes looked up.

Ah trust of beauty and discipline,
win me to wait, leaning on wheel
till feel of distance, cosmic rest
bursts from that bush of traffic glow.
Know how the driven, flagging hate,
the lateness, panic, haste to be foiled,
in soil of patient moment fades,
to raise red quince of heaven's bush
in hush before the traffic moves.

How does the poem avoid the outworn, the didactic? A distinctively contemporary sense-object, a commonplace substance of the mechanical age, is related to nature and to the religious experience. What does "till feel of distance, cosmic rest" imply? Man's kinship with the cosmic and his intuitive reliance upon it. The here-and-now are joined with the divine, the mystical, but the poem attempts to present its theme *indirectly*, without any didactic or conclusive statement. By the technique of indirection, by cumulative hints and nuances, the poem asserts: "Christ lives in the traffic light, and through its delicate precision of timing, disciplines us to accept his timelessness, teaches us that concepts of delay and frustration, partition and division are not real, that trust in his spaceless infinite goodness is the only measure — mathematical and scientific as well as spiritual — of actual being and doing."

Here is another brief poem which explores the cosmic idea through the use of excellent indirection. It is Richard Wilbur's THE DEATH OF A TOAD.

A toad the power mower caught,
Chewed and clipped of a leg, with a hobbling hop has got
　To the garden verge, and sanctuaried him
　Under the cineraria leaves, in the shade
　　Of the ashen heartshaped leaves, in a dim,
　　　Low, and a final glade.

　The rare original heartsblood goes,
Spends on the earthen hide, in the folds of wizenings, flows
　In the gutters of the banked and staring eyes. He lies
　As still as if he would return to stone,
　　And soundlessly attending, dies
　　　Toward some deep monotone,

　　Toward misted and ebullient seas
And cooling shores, toward lost Amphibia's emperies.
　Day dwindles, drowning, and at length is gone
　In the wide and antique eyes, which still appear
　　To watch, across the castrate lawn,
　　　The haggard daylight steer.

What does this poem have to do with religion or the cosmic? What is the author trying to tell us? Well, by indirection
we are told: All life, human or animal, is related to and derives from the same sources. And, by inference, the death of
anything in the natural realm is the death of the mortal also
— for we are all natural. "Toward some deep monotone, /
Toward misted and ebullient seas / And cooling shores,
toward lost Amphibia's emperies."

And beyond this, what does the death of the toad mean?
The poet, by implication, draws us back toward original and
primitive beginnings, through the stages of evolution, not only
anthropological, but spiritual. "Rare original heartsblood . . .
Toward misted and ebullient seas / And cooling shores" gives
the effect of comfort more than the sensual; "lost Amphibia's

emperies" suggests the ideal, a metaphysical absolute. We exercise an identification with the process, the essential growth of life itself, the hunger of life, mortal and animal, to *return* to its source — yearning toward Him, a fulfillment through suffering, as, in this case, through the very pain of death.

In turning backward with sadness and longing, the toad rediscovers self in eternity, moving, as does human life in death, toward a new stage in infinite evolution, evolving toward what may be the mutuality, sanctity, and equality of all life. We are all part of beginnings, a binding love, implies the author, that goes much further back than this world ("rare original heartsblood"), and that is our unifying, cosmic heritage ("some deep monotone").

Why then is THE DEATH OF A TOAD successful? Chiefly because the enormous compassion of the author communicates itself throughout, evoking a response in the reader. Compassion is at the heart of religion. Instilled in most of us as a moral faculty involving the redemptive hopes of man, human or divine, it operates, consciously or unconsciously, in whatever we do. Thus, the reader of poetry instinctively reaches for this element — "and *sanctuaried* him . . . in the shade / Of the ashen heartshaped leaves, in a dim, / Low and final glade . . ." And again: "The rare original heartsblood goes . . . soundlessly attending . . . In the wide and antique eyes, which still appear / To watch, across the castrate lawn, / The haggard daylight steer." Time, says the author, the coming and going of daylight, is dwarfed by the patience, the psychic watching of living creatures, even in death — watching for what? For the ideal "empery" which appears "lost" now, but is still in God's (evolution's) hand, to be delivered to us, to all life, in his good time. And "sanctuaried" conveys the idea of the sanctity of life, the divine nature of this destiny — for the toad (all manner of being), as for all people.

100

Indirection, we see now, has much to do with the accomplishment. But other techniques of the modern poet, analyzed earlier, have also contributed: diction and imagery that are bold, shocking — "gutters of the banked and staring eyes . . . the castrate lawn . . . haggard daylight steer . . .;" rhythm and sound that penetrate and capture, form that rises and falls like the expiring pulse of the toad.

In THE DEATH OF A TOAD we find the modern religious poem in which the private psyche lends its gifts to social vision, one that integrates man at a subconscious level with his inherent and noble ends and with meanings beyond time. But if man feels profound sympathy for all life, what of the primal power that created this vessel of sympathy? What of the pitying love and mercy of God Himself? Let us turn briefly to a contemporary treatment of this idea in Lawrence Holmes' RUTH FOR THE MORTAL, written in Sapphics, a traditional but still vital form:

> Earthworm — delving lonely with sentient finger
> Deep in loamy corridors, cool, uncharted —
> Knows with single delicate sense each lightless
>   Intricate earthway.

> Bees, that sip and savor the clover's cordial,
> Dwell in Eden — innocent Eves, ecstatic —
> Tasting not the fruit, but the unforbidden
>   Nectar of Knowledge.

> Birds on wing look down on the emerald forests,
> Seeing these as velvety shadeless mosses.
> Mites in lichens prowl as in Congo jungles,
>   Hemmed by the vine-snarls.

101

Mind eternal — spaceless, without horizon,
Probing Possibility — fashions creatures,
Myriad, fragile, each with its destined special
    Finite perspective.

We are His antennae, His eyes and tasters.
Thus He may ubiquitous range, All-knowing —
Move, perceive, and love, on the scale of every
    Animate earthling.

So by watching man at the soul's arena,
Present at our clashes of flesh and spirit,
May He learn, in throes of the human drama,
    Ruth for the mortal!

The perspective has shifted, but Holmes conveys the same idea of mystical hunger and solicitude that has been caught by Wilbur in THE DEATH OF A TOAD. Compare it to what Hemingway does in *The Old Man and the Sea*. Through his own compassion, Hemingway reveals that bond of compassion that exists among all creatures: the old man for the gallant fish, the boy for both, and, by implication, *the sympathy of God working through them for every being He has made*. That same great force of tender, comprehending love of life which we find in Hemingway encompasses Holmes' poem, and comes out of the sources that bore the toad, *the pitying and merciful sources*. What do these ideas add up to? We might call it "brotherhood" — a very outworn word — not only brotherhood among men, but between man and nature, and between man and all life — species here and in unlimited universes, all origins and ends. Or we may prefer to name it "unity."

And yet, is the concept of brotherhood enough? May we not also *perform* the *act* of mercy? Let us take a poem, brilliantly modern in every way, to illustrate this idea: THE FISH by Elizabeth Bishop:

I caught a tremendous fish
and held him beside the boat
half out of water, with my hook
fast in a corner of his mouth.
He didn't fight.
He hadn't fought at all.
He hung a grunting weight,
battered and venerable
and homely. Here and there
his brown skin hung in strips
like ancient wall-paper,
and its pattern of darker brown
was like wall-paper:
shapes like full-blown roses
stained and lost through age.
He was speckled with barnacles,
fine rosettes of lime,
and infested
with tiny white sea-lice,
and underneath two or three
rags of green weed hung down.
While his gills were breathing in
the terrible oxygen
— the frightening gills,
fresh and crisp with blood,
that can cut so badly —
I thought of the coarse white flesh
packed in like feathers,
the big bones and the little bones,
the dramatic reds and blacks
of his shiny entrails,
and the pink swim-bladder
like a big peony.

I looked into his eyes
which were far larger than mine
but shallower, and yellowed,
the irises backed and packed
with tarnished tinfoil
seen through lenses
of old scratched isinglass.
They shifted a little, but not
to return my stare.
— It was more like the tipping
of an object toward the light.
I admired his sullen face,
the mechanism of his jaw,
and then I saw
that from his lower lip
— if you could call it a lip —
grim, wet, and weapon-like,
hung five old pieces of fish-line,
or four and a wire leader
with the swivel still attached,
with all their five big hooks
grown firmly in his mouth.
A green line, frayed at the end
where he broke it, two heavier lines,
and a fine black thread
still crimped from the strain and snap
when it broke and he got away.
Like medals with their ribbons
frayed and wavering,
a five-haired beard of wisdom
trailing from his aching jaw.
I stared and stared
and victory filled up
the little rented boat,
from the pool of bilge

where oil had spread a rainbow
around the rusted engine
to the bailer rusted orange,
the sun-cracked thwarts,
the oarlocks on their strings,
the gunnels — until everything
was rainbow, rainbow, rainbow!
And I let the fish go.

What kind of poem is it that moves us most? It is the one that stirs us at that psychic-ethical depth where we live most intensely, and the one — provided it is of equal technical merit to those written at other levels — that potentially will give most and live longest.

Richard Wilbur shows us that compassion is the *sine qua non* of a sensitive human being. Reverence and sympathy infuse his poem ("and sanctuaried him / Under the cineraria leaves, in the shade / Of the ashen heartshaped leaves, in a dim, / Low, and final glade"). But pity and love, declares Elizabeth Bishop, must issue in the act. Where Hemingway's Old Man feels sympathy, a kinship with the fish, but can only kill it, Elizabeth Bishop is moved to release the creature at her mercy. It is this peculiar spirit — the will to translate pity or compassion into an act — breaking through all form and technique, that persists as a cardinal criterion of the best verse, past or present. Young Wordsworth possessed the mark of this mercy, and the compassion-into-deed ennobled Blake and reverberated in Whitman.

The two modern poems of Mr. Wilbur and Miss Bishop — the drab and sordid death of the toad, the triumphant life-force of a scarred and dauntless fish and his liberation through understanding — exalt us to the highest planes of poetic experience.

6

Poem and Poet

"How does a poem begin?" "How is it created?" One of the first questions an audience asks a poet is likely to involve the process of creation.

But there are almost as many ways of getting words on paper as there are artists to be asked.

Brewster Ghiselin, in his book, *The Creative Process,* cites such divergent figures as Einstein, Mozart, Henry Miller, Yeats, Jung, Kipling, and D. H. Lawrence as highly creative people who have testified that their great moments of revelation, of achievement, were subconscious and spontaneous, coming without deliberate effort at times when the mind was at ease. Many of us recognize that below the surface the mind often works best, when the individual is not forcing it — as we go about other activities and involvements. Nearly all of us have had the experience of forgetting a name, a meaning, an event, and the harder we try consciously to recall it the more it escapes us — until, placing the problem in the subconscious, the answer may suddenly burst forth later when we least expect it. By extension, there in the subconscious, in the dark, unbeknownst, the creative mind may produce the nearly finished job, to a large extent polished and perfected; then when the artist calls upon it, or when it is ready — without being asked — it thrusts itself upward into the daylight of his attention.

Whether, like this, the poem bursts forth without conscious effort, or is the result of long and intensive labor, depends, quite naturally, upon the artist. The more deliberate poet, who revises freely and often, might describe with complete validity the process by which he produces a satisfying work of art. On the other hand, the present writer must of necessity be personal and subjective in his own evaluation of the creative process as it directly involves the poet-at-work.

Seldom, if ever, do I think about a poem until it begins to sound in the mind in actual words, with that peculiar pitch, accent, shading of secret, inner sound which varies with each writer. It is not the concept so much as the image or tonal quality that moves me, and the poem, once completed — often in twenty or forty-five minutes — is usually put aside as a keen, momentary pleasure and forgotten.

Seldom is there deliberate application of my mind to the end result; there is no premeditation, no over-all plan, no formalized scaffolding of thematic concern. These things are allowed to attack from ambush, with the mind kept in a state of rest most of the day, or often deliberately made blank — void — the main purpose being to relax it, not to urge or cudgel it to compose something. And when, suddenly, the words have formed themselves — without effort or coercion — in the subconscious mind, to shape meaningful images, they begin to enunciate in the conscious mind, to sound their music

107

— usually when I am engaged in other pursuits — and they emerge with tremendous compulsion. They are set down almost intact, and if an occasional word is changed here or there, it is only because of an effort to record exactly what has already been *done* for me, rather than my *doing* anything to alter the image or wording received. After the forty-five minutes or so required to complete the job thoroughly at the first sitting, rarely do I return to alter a word; and if so, more often than not, the first choice was the best. As one critic remarked, "It is as if the concept and the execution happened simultaneously."

Although relying heavily on the subconscious and its dictates as to what a poem shall be and when it shall erupt, there is one deliberate way in which emergence from the cocoon may be facilitated. If a given day comes when there is time to write, but no immediate rush of words fills the void, I may sit at a desk (or lie down for greater composure), letting the mind go — but in a definite, guided direction — *backwards, as far back as possible*. A conscious effort may be necessary to put it in a receptive mood, to allow images of earlier years — particularly of childhood or adolescence — to crystallize and take hold. An image may have appeared before, perhaps vaguely, but never consciously considered; or it may be one obscured by time, one that has been beating for years at the portals of consciousness — or perhaps an apparently meaningless picture that nevertheless has some personal significance. Encouraging the prevalent image to sharpen and grow, I write it down, whether then or later, when it is revived in the consciousness. No effort is made to explain it, or even understand it, but merely to delineate precisely the vision itself and the details of its imagery.

In other words, the subconscious is loaded with images trying to reach us, trying to tell us something we ought to know,

108

for our moral well-being or development, physical health, or esthetic pleasure. The deeper down and further back we go, to uncover these symbols, the more effective, significant, and powerful they are. As Wordsworth pointed out, the child is nearer to God, having just arrived from Him, "trailing clouds of glory." Thus, the earlier and fresher the experiences we can recapture, through exploration of the involuntary image or symbol, the better. What seems irrational or wild often proves to be — as in the high moments of Coleridge or Dylan Thomas — the poet's best work.

What of this process as it applies to the specific act of composition? For this discussion we will consider the genesis of two poems; both were written with speed and intensity, but the composition of the first, while spontaneous, was more directly revealed; the other was the result of a subconscious, psychological approach — an experiment in dream-poetry. Let us examine the first approach in detail.

Seated at my desk one day — no words coming of their own volition — I directed my mental focus back in time — back, back, back to childhood — and, relaxing, allowed whatever image might be so inclined to emerge. The psychologist might have called it a "permissive frame of mind."

And then, a strange, a weird experience. There was the cold, bleak, impoverished parsonage in the New Hampshire village where I had lived till the age of eight; there was my father, the indigent, shabby country parson, kneeling in deep snow in front of the parsonage, at the top of an embankment down which I had skied as a boy. The embankment was drifted deep, and snow was falling heavily. And then, an odd detail: On my father's back — his shoulder blades, to be exact — was a pair of snowshoes, which he was trying to reach for and pull off. And next, awareness of something even more

109

astonishing: The snowshoes were not wood and rawhide; they were human flesh, part of his body. And the harder he tried to tear them free — the sweat pouring from him — the less he could move them. And there, at the foot of the snowy embankment, was the field where I used to play Cowboys-and-Indians; the drifts came right to the bottom of the embankment, to the edge of the field, — snow five feet in depth; but the field itself — miracle of miracles! — was in full springtime bloom; the flowers were blowing in the wind, the apple trees were blossoming handsomely. Clad in an Indian suit, I was running across that warm, sweet-scented, sunny field to the woods I had used as a boyhood hiding-place to watch the trout in their pools and think private thoughts.

And so, one half of the village, where my father knelt, was in the grip of a blizzard; the other half, where the boy was running to some new adventure in those secret woods, was at Maytime's climax of loveliness. What a peculiar image! Without stopping to analyze it, I merely assigned it to the subconscious and forgot about it entirely.

Weeks later, in a moment of relaxation one morning, the image returned — this time with much greater compulsion. The subliminal mind had chosen the words, achieved the task; the lines were all there, and in half an hour the poem was written. HORIZON THONG:

> Go back now; pause to mark
> that hill town cut in two:
> one half, green summer's charm,
> the other, chasmed in snow.
>
> Horizon, a thong of red
> knotted by smoldering sun;
> wind, the wind in the drifts,
> and crystal blossoms flung

downward — so near, so warm —
to where orchards bend and lift.

And father, — father who kneels
to pull snowshoes from his back,
looks down to the shining field
where his son runs, easy and fast;

he must follow, follow to save,
but the snowshoes will not free;
they are rooted to shoulder blade,
they are flesh of paternity.

Only a quick run down,
but helpless he kneels in cold,
watches his young boy run
over meadows lyric and full
toward woods, a woods of his own.

Wrenching, and wet with pain,
the father downward bows;
the village of homes and men
grows faint in the blizzard's glow.

The boy flashes under trees
and fades. The horizon mark
binds throat of man on his knees;
the sun-knot tightens to dark.

The attitude in this poem, if memory serves, was never
consciously held at all — that a father suffers because he
cannot continue, beyond a certain point, to accompany his
son in his growing up; that the boy must depart and become
a different self and develop on his own. Never do I recall
having discussed such a topic with anyone. Yet, year by year,

there must have been a growing subconscious awareness that my own father had felt this way, and suddenly it sprang torrentially into the light.

Disciplines, acquired through experience and practice, play their part, of course, in achieving the end result — techniques we have considered previously, while examining other contemporary poetry. The major effect of the poem lies in the contrast of scenes and in the uniqueness of the father's predicament. The image is central, contributing to the odd, dreamlike atmosphere, which plays a particularly important role. "Horizon a thong of red / knotted by smoldering sun" presents the unreal, mystical mood which carries beyond the rational and gives the poem its individuality. The rhythm is quick — trimeter — almost like a hurried breath, to suggest dramatic tension, the urgency of the father's need to follow his son, the horror at realizing that parenthood, which demands closeness to a growing child, must require a fatal tearing away of the self. The rapidity of metre also conveys the running of the boy, the swift strokes of the blizzard, and the merciless passing of time against which the father cannot prevail.

The rhymes, though fairly close, are impulsive here and there — in keeping with the greater freedom from absolute form in modern verse — and to emphasize the pace and the sense of lyric, uninhibited springtime. The diction attempts a realism of detail and stringency of tempo that may be considered more contemporary than traditional: "chasmed in snow," "the sun-knot tightens to dark." This has a hard, almost staccato quality.

And there is indirection: much is left to the reader to infer, not only part by part — for example, he is unsure of the significance of the father in that odd situation — but also in terms of the meaning of the whole poem, which he must approach in a roundabout way. He must supply *his* version of its significance, once the symbols and their relationships have mingled and shaped their impact.

What is the importance of this last factor, in considering HORIZON THONG? The poem is symbolic, a fantasy, rising straight from its long gestation in the subconscious world. The key symbol for the poem was found, we recall, by drifting back into the far past and letting it emerge. This kind of poem tries to re-create a state of being, recording only the *distillation* of an experience through symbol, and allowing each reader to make his own interpretation. As such, it communicates itself differently to different people, and the reactions are varied. For example, the first three persons who read it had these divergent reactions: The first said it was a poem about the father looking back on his childhood; another said it was written from the viewpoint of the child experiencing the loss of his father; the third commented that it was essentially the nostalgia of the author looking back at his youth.

What happens when the poet goes beyond even the spontaneous-subconscious act of creation and composes a poem from the very dream itself? In this context, let us consider the following comments by the late psychologist, C. G. Jung, in an issue of *Tomorrow:*

". . . A very modern form of psychology — analytical or complex psychology — envisages the possibility of there being certain processes in the unconscious which, by virtue of their symbolism, compensate the defects . . . of the conscious attitude . . . . Dreams, fantasies, and psychoses produce images to all appearances identical with mythological motifs of which the individuals concerned had absolutely no knowledge, not even indirect knowledge acquired through popular figures of speech or through the symbolic language of the Bible . . . . Whatever the structure of the unconscious may be, one thing is certain: it contains an indefinite number of motifs or patterns of an archaic character, in principle identical with the root ideas of mythology and similar thought forms . . . .

"An introverted attitude, therefore, which withdraws its emphasis from the external world (the world of consciousness) and localizes it in the subjective factor (the background of consciousness) necessarily calls forth the characteristic manifestations of the unconscious, namely, archaic thought forms imbued with 'ancestral' or 'historic' feeling, and, beyond them, the sense of indefiniteness, timelessness, oneness. The extraordinary feeling of oneness is a common experience in all forms of 'mysticism.'

"Formerly, men called the gods unfavorable; now we prefer to call it a neurosis, and we seek the cause in lack of vitamins, in endocrine disturbance, overwork, or sex. The co-operation of the unconscious, which is something we never think of and always take for granted, is, when it suddenly fails, a very serious matter indeed."

What happens when Dr. Jung's remarks are applied to the poetic experience — if a poem is placed in the nimbus of subconscious (or unconscious) clarity, this "ancestral," "historic" feeling, the sense of "oneness" he refers to? Could it become a more valid poem — sharper, more universal, and, according to our idea-range of values, more compassionate, encompassing a deed of mercy as in Elizabeth Bishop's THE FISH?

Today, psychiatry, physical therapy, economic panaceas, better and bigger diversions — all of which are being attempted with greater and greater urgency — are symbols of modern man's failure to find mental health and balance. Is it that we fail because we seek to adjust to the outward world to the exclusion of the deeply inward, the world of the visionary, or preternatural — what Aldous Huxley calls the antipodes, or Mind-At-Large — a half-world between the fixed and humdrum realities of everyday existence and those enormous sweeps of all-things-in-their-essential-being?

That subliminal realm where we can be released and purified has been the spiritual domain of such notable poets as Donne, Blake, de la Mare, Wordsworth, Coleridge, Poe, and Dickinson. They were able to heal others, to purge and exalt because they wrote symbolically: they crossed over and took us with them into the nuances of ultimate reality, the subtleties, elusive fragrances, colors and stunning beauty, the unexpected and daring images that shift and change and flourish beyond rational meaning, and yet remain the same imperishably.

Of all the arts, poetry, combining music and the imagery of painting, can be the most self-releasing, the greatest therapy. In an article "An Ulcer, Gentlemen, is an Unwritten Poem," the eminent poet John Ciardi wrote:

"Poetry and practicality are in fact two different worlds with two different orders of experience and of imagination. The poet enters his world as an *as if*: he writes *as if* he were analyzing a real man seated before him. He is free with a stroke of the pen to change the lineaments of the world he has imagined. The practical man has no such large freedom. He enters a world called *is*. When he is at work, he *is* plowing a field, he *is* assembling chemical apparatus, he *is* interviewing an actual man . . . . (But) the fact is . . . that only the *as if* of the vicarious imagination has a place in the final mind of man . . . .

"An ulcer, gentlemen, is an unkissed imagination taking its revenge for having been jilted. It is an unwritten poem, a neglected music, an unpainted watercolor, an undanced dance. It is a declaration from the mankind of the man that a clear spring of joy has not been tapped, and that it must break through, muddily, on its own. Poetry is one of the forms of joy, the most articulate, the most expanding, and, therefore, the most fulfilling form. It is no separation from the world; it is the mankind of the world."

Here, then, is another paradox: this "mankind-of-the-world" poetry, which men need for their own healing, is not of this world; it is the limbo, the exquisite adumbration of strange color and sound, the half-world and outpost of the imagination, where our illusions of *here* merge with our vision of the *wherever*.

George Copeland, in an article "Debussy, the Man I Knew," recalled that:

"Musically, Debussy felt himself to be a kind of auditory 'sensitve.' He not only heard sounds that no other ear was able to register, but he found a way of expressing things that are not customarily said. He had an almost fanatical conviction that a musical score does not begin with a composer, but that it emerges out of space, through centuries of time, passes before him, and goes on, fading into the distance (as it came) with no sense of finality."

The same may be true of the life span of our human race, and our place in it — individual, friend, family, lover. It has all happened already, and at times our perceptive selves flick aside the shutter and behold what has always been there. Yet even then we do not understand rationally as much as we feel and comprehend intuitively.

With this in mind, let us turn to our second example of composition, the result of an experiment in recounting dreams in poetry. It began with my keeping a pencil and paper handy at night and jotting down phrases to cover the significant details of a dream, which, weeks later, might act as the core of a poem. A psychologist who had been conducting experiments with the dreams of college students was intrigued by the project and suggested exploring the possibilities of using certain psychological and psychoanalytic techniques to discover whether the meanings of these poems, inspired by dreams, could be enriched by such techniques. Specifically, my free associations to all images in the poem were assembled (the images had been scrambled so as to minimize the cues from the sequence of images as they appeared in the poem), and the series of poems was then examined for recurrent themes, levels of meaning, and so forth.

What the psychologist found was that "because of compression and the poet's art, a single poem of this extra-reality sort conveys the condition of our time better than an entire book in the field of psychology." One of the strongest recurring themes in these dream poems was "man's isolation from his fellow-man," his inability to communicate his actual self in our mechanized world. Let us now turn to a poem in which this theme is central, and the writing of which gave me the same unearthly, super-rational, already-done-for-you mystical sense, described in the paragraph about Debussy. A poem called THE GARAGE:

I kept telephoning the repairman at the garage. "Explain:
when will my car be ready?" And yet there,
staring out of a phone-booth, I stood, — there
in the very garage I was telephoning to.

"My dog," I said. "My luggage. Are they
safe? Locked in? What was wrong? Why
did I leave the car?"

The garageman's voice, thin and far, cracked like a celluloid
toy.   I couldn't hear a word.

I hurried from the booth.   The garage had many levels.
I kept striding down, down, searching.
There were burning-black cables and ancient cars being
        raised;
straining men held up cylinder-blocks.
I pushed through dangling cables and chains;
crazed, I sought everywhere, I ran.
But none was the repairman, none my car.
Wherever it stood, helpless and spent,
my dog was inside, all
my belongings.

I flung myself into another booth; my voice
boiled in the mouthpiece, under the close roof, like scalding
water: "Which part
of the garage are you in?
Is it fixed?   The dog, you say, is gone?
The luggage was never there?"

I stared through my sweat, past
the scratched and grimy phone-booth glass; and tall
and horrifying hung cranes and chains and cables,
a forest through which
the click of the repairman's voice seemed to come,
humming into the phone over long wire, too far,
too tired.   "I can't tell you how to get
to this level.   I don't know what's wrong with your car.
The doors are unlocked and the luggage and dog
are gone."

Not long after the publication of this poem, one reader
made a comment that perhaps amplifies this aspect of our

discussion of poem and poet: "There are glimpses of insight which may come to one in an instant, in dreams, or almost as a mystic experience. How to express these or to glean the intuition they represent except by poetry? It may reveal that there is a knowledge — rarely unearthed — in the mind which is universal and cannot be learned. Poetry must serve as the medium to communicate this to others, since we ourselves are isolated and cannot convey this knowledge in prosaic terms. One is aware at once that the poem is a dream; the symbols cannot be rationally explained, yet there is a feeling of communication which is inexpressible, which defies explanation. On the other hand, explanation may not be necessary."

This reaction tells us something about the modern poet in relation to himself. It is through an experiment such as this that the poet may ascertain more of his own nature, his individuality, *and* the community of experience with all men, through the spontaneous and released expression of the unconscious; through dream poetry or other similar innovations; through a therapy of self that encompasses the healing of others, their aesthetic excitement, spiritual adventure, and self-discovery.

7

Poem and Reader

WE HAVE EXAMINED contemporary poetry in its multiple aspects — image and diction, sound patterns, form, idea, feeling, and in some of its creative implications. We have seen some of the ways in which a modern poem is distinguishable — what makes it modern.

As we have noted earlier, poetry has lost ground during the past few decades because it has been overdogmatized, overintellectualized, and, like many American children, overpampered, overmedicated, and overprotected.

Poetry belongs to people.

While, for the purposes of this book, we have had to dissect it, poetry, properly, should not — cannot — be pigeonholed or labelled; it must flow out of the appreciator as well as the propagator, spontaneously, and always amazingly.

Not long ago, a verse magazine was launched which carried the militant slogan: "Clarity, sanity, simplicity!" Clarity

120

for whom? Many of the greatest poems are clear only after centuries, and even then only to a critical few. What is clear to one person is not clear to another, and *complexity is often the strength of a poem,* not because it is achieved deliberately, but because the more profound its nature, the more complex it is.

Can any good poem be reduced to a slogan or definition? Why should it be oversimplified? Poetry, the most exalting — yet most elusive — of the arts, must be let alone to burst forth, unexpected and inexplicable. We can only hope to recognize it when it happens. And one way to recognize it is to encourage every effort *at* recognition, every effort *at* perception — at every level.

Poetry should require continuity, a permanent relationship between author and reader. *A poem is not complete until it is responded to;* there is no author without audience; the creative art is a reciprocal and simultaneous *doing between the two.* Each interpretation is essential, part of the *creative making, reality,* and *being* of the poem. ·We may refer to it as *poetry-in-the-round.* Without audience, or the *co-maker,* the work of art exists in a vacuum.

There are as many poems in each composition as there are reactions to it. The so-called "author" merely triggers the cooperative process, the multiplicity of truth and meaning that adds up to the eventual unity of the poem — its place in society.

A respected poet and critic once wrote me: "A poem, like anything, is all the ways it can be seen, while it remains what it is. I should be interested in the coexistence of delicate slowness and delicate speed in a poem. There are, in poems, picture and logic; there are ease and discontent. In the same way as human beings, when they feel understood,

121

feel they are being seen in every way they can be seen, so if a poem were a person, it would look for an instantaneous and coherent diversity of being seen. This is hard to get at."

Hard to get at, perhaps, but impossible? Another authority on poetry stated: "Only a few poems can survive dissection, and I cannot contemplate 'three interpretive slants' without pitying the poet subjected to the triple surgery."

Yet ten minds interpret a poem in ten different ways, a fact of life which some critics refuse to face because they believe there are unshakable standards — namely their own. "All criticism is individual taste," Stephen Vincent Benét once said. Minds diverge widely in reaction to poetry; often the poet intends something different from the reader's response (if he can ever actually determine *what* he intends, for his *post facto* ideas are often forced and untrue when he tries to return and recall what was alive in him during composition). The keenest readers respond independently, each with his own reaction-truth and his right to it. Two keen critical minds coming to, say, a Frost poem, might have equally sensitive — but different — reactions.

Not long ago, a teachers'-college workshop of mine in New England applied these theories of interpretation, of spontaneity and the release of the subconscious, at various age levels. The report of that project noted: "Today there is a growing awareness that we need more vital self-expression to ease the tensions created by the confusing pace at which we live. The value of music and painting, in the treatment of the mentally ill, has universal acceptance. The therapeutic value of poetry, *for everybody,* deserves similar recognition. Of all the arts, it may have the greatest power to release subconscious conflict.

"The best poetry from earliest times has been subconsciously, not consciously, written. Poets have expressed themselves *under compulsion* to relieve inner tension. If poetry has power to heal the poet, it can also heal the reader. To achieve this, however, the reader must do more than try to comprehend the poet's intended meaning. People often react to a poem with a simple, 'I don't get it.' Actually, the poem should 'get the reader.' This, though, for many people, opens a new dimension in poetry-reading. No two people have the same reactions to a painting, musical composition, or poem. The important thing is for everyone to free himself of restraint so that his own reaction can be full and deep, drawing upon his richest imaginative powers. The interpreters are the co-makers of the poem.

"We all know how Shakespeare means more to us at forty than he did at twenty. His work changes as we change. Thus the poet alters in respect to his own poetry, and his readers alter with him. The conditions of their lives shift, and if we could register their complete view of one poem every given minute for a week, we would find constant modification. (Each of my poems changes every day, every hour. My audience make their own poetry from mine; I from theirs; we grow together.) Poetry becomes *process*. Poetry becomes organic, *community* experience."

In interpreting poetry, age makes little difference. Often, the younger the person, the more astonishing, profound, and exciting the response.

To illustrate, let us take a single poem and look at some interpretations gleaned at the same poetry workshop. A poem of mine called, THE BOOK:

I came to the margin of yesterday:
I saw a girl on the edge of flowers.
There were birds on a steeple, and clouds as high
as the stars of childhood in mystery's tower.

A gray stone library, red of roof,
stood by a sidewalk where people were small
but excessively kind, and their voices drew
the fish from the water, the fox from the hill.

The girl on the edge of the flowers stood deep,
so deep in the grass I saw only her head
and a bare arm held high.   She looked rosy and sweet.
Then I saw what she held — a book she had read,
far down in the insects, the drowsing, the pollen.
The words she had read shone like drops on her brow
and glowed on her lips, and exquisitely shone
in eyes blue-eternal and gray here-and-now;

and from library windows, heads were thrust out,
the steeple birds paused, and the clouds swung low;
the fox raised his head, the fish made no sound;
the flowers were diamonds from the darkest
        unknown.

Let's begin with two adult reactions from members of the
teachers' workshop, the first by a young man:

"The Book holds for me the stimulation of an impressionistic painting. One is attracted by its opening line, 'I came
to the margin,' which reminds us that the closest we can come
to any yesterday is by way of thoughtful longing. The use of
light upon the setting achieves clarity, a quiet warm total
effect. Part of the harmony lies in the choice of words such
as 'gray stone library' — the internal silence of the building,
implied but not stated. . . . Everything combines to produce
a quickening, a realization of having experienced something
similar, which becomes important to our later periods of reflection; but the real excitement comes about by seeing it
recorded *as you would like to have it told.*"

The second interpretation is by a woman schoolteacher: "Certain books, by their ethereal passages, make us feel as though we were floating in space. The 'small people, excessively kind,' are our authors who have truly drawn 'the fish from the water, the fox from the hill,' by the magic of their accounts. . . . Nothing is too small or insignificant, that, well written about, will not live forever."

Here, then, are two interpretations, different, yet equally authentic, because both are sincere, pointing to the theory that there are as many poems in each composition as there are reactions to it.

In the past, poetry in the classroom has largely meant boring memorization of the works of the old masters. Instead of developing an appreciation and love for this medium of expression, students have responded with antipathy. They have felt no kinship, no stimulation, no self-realization. They have come to believe, as one ten-year-old boy expressed it when a teacher told him she was taking a course with a modern poet, who was interested in having youngsters like him write down their reactions to his verses: "Why, I thought all poets were dead!"

This author-audience method of interpretation offers an entirely new approach for teachers working with pupils of all ages. Here the student is allowed to tell in his own words how the poem makes him feel, what pictures he sees, what thoughts are aroused. He is creating as truly in his own way as the poet who wrote the poem. If some *one* new thought, or idea, or remembrance, or dream is awakened in his mind, then the poem has achieved its purpose, a new dimension has been reached. In turn, the poet gains an enlarged perspective of his own work; he and his reader share a common experience from which each derives growth and new freedom.

125

Reactions to THE BOOK by seventeen-year-olds differed greatly from those of the adults. First, that of a teenage boy, a prep-school student: "Men are uninformed about the world's mysteries. We are like the fish and fox in our ignorance. It seems that the more we read and know, the more confounded we become."

And from another boy of about the same age:

"The girl struck me as having reached a turning point in her life, the change from adolescence to maturity. 'The margin of yesterday' I took as possibly meaning the termination of her childhood. Up to now she had lounged in ignorance of life, reading the book of learning until she could get up and face the world. Up to now she was hidden in the grasses among the insects and tiny creatures, and the buildings were so tall and the clouds so high. Now, having learned enough, she rises out of the grass and is seen above the grass with her new knowledge written on her face as a sign of maturity."

Finally, let us consider reactions to the same poem by a group of ten-year-old pupils, most of them sixth-graders. The teacher merely had them read the poem, after reading it to them herself, and then asked for the instantaneous effect it had on them. They were not allowed to communicate with each other or receive outside help. When asked to write down what she thought the poet was trying to say, one little girl protested:

"But I thought *you* were supposed to tell us that!"

Thus was their concept of poetry to be revolutionized. Listening to the results of this change, this shifting of responsibility and meaning to the shoulders of each young reader, recalls Lloyd Frankenburg's comment that "the child is the poet in each of us, the part that responds to vision."

First, Karen, a ten-year-old girl, wrote:

"The girl in the meadows was happy. She had just read a book on God's creation, and she was glad that she could be with what God had made. All these people were looking out of the library to see why the girl was so happy, as though they were part of the book. When the people did this, it made the meadow quiet. The animals knew they were in God's world, and they hushed so they could be sure that they were not doing wrong. The people on the sidewalk were small. They were not as big as God, but they were very kind. They made the fox and the fish draw near to hear them."

Next, the reaction of Paul, a boy the same age: "I thought of a man reminiscing of his home town and the girl he loved. She was as beautiful as flowers, and was a girl who loved everyone and everything. Whatever she said, all people heard. The book meant that she was the spirit of knowledge, and through books he could learn about nature, the stars, and the kindness of people."

Gary, a fifth-grade boy wrote: "The girl in the garden is either small or the plants are very tall. And I think the insects in the garden are quiet because they are watching the girl. When the poem said, 'The words she had read shone like drops on her brow,' I think that it meant that what she had read she was thinking about over and over again."

And from Carol, in the sixth grade: "It came to dusk or nightfall of yesterday. You saw a girl standing near the place where the flowers were. A steeple is high and clouds are high in the sky and you don't know what is in the child's mind. It's a mystery to everyone except the child. The reason why they say 'birds in the steeple and clouds high' is because they want you to think of something tall or maybe even bright. You don't really know the child in his or her mind. They use the expression, 'draw the fish from the water' and 'the fox from the hill,' to express the quality of their voices. They didn't actually draw the fish from the water and the fox from the hill. They wanted you to know that their voices were something worthwhile mentioning so they use those expressions. She wasn't really so deep in the grass that you only saw her head. This was to show her thought: it was a *deep* thought. . . . Everything grew very quiet, for nightfall appeared, and it must have been a beautiful evening with stars shining brightly in the marvelous heavens above where mysteries still are."

Another girl named Carol said: "I think this poem means that years ago birds and the people and other things used to be peaceful and there was not so much racket. You used to see flowers that weren't trampled down. The girl was so quiet reading her book and the insects so drowsy resting so peacefully. Now everybody's running and jumping about. I think the author would like to go back to his childhood town."

Pamela wrote: "My impression of this poem is that a person is getting older and he remembers his childhood sweetheart, the freshness of her youth blossoming more beautifully in his mind than the spring flowers. Her eyes were like stars, and her words shone like jewels in his memory. . . . Then suddenly everything he had been thinking of seemed to shine very brightly, but all of a sudden everything seemed to stop; the birds no longer sang, the clouds swung low, the people stopped and looked. Suddenly he knew that it was an old picture in his mind dreaming of the past, and he knew that all the dreaming in the world would never let him live his childhood again."

Bill felt this way: "The sun is turning pinkish red, on this late summer day. The flowers are glowing, the clouds are lowing. It is getting later now. A girl stands reading, in a yellow meadow. A fox starts howling from the green hills. The clouds are turning pink. The sun is backing away under the green hills. People are talking in the library. . . . You can see the steeple birds pause and look. The fox stops howling, the girl stops reading, kind people stop reading in the library, and they start staring. Night has arrived."

Is it any wonder that the poet, who merely wrote down the words in the beginning, finds the horizon of his poems widening with each new interpretation? Perhaps one can see now how poetry can be shared, can become a part of community activity and enjoyment. No matter how varied, how extended or brief the thoughts and feelings in response to a poem may be, they are part of the history of the art; for all of them, exactly as much as the words the author put down, help make the poem itself and serve to complete the poetic experience.

Glossary

Note: The following has no pretensions to being a complete glossary of poetic terminology, but is appended here as a handy reference to the more technical terms used in portions of this book.

ALEXANDRINE. A line of poetry consisting of six metrical (iambic) feet.

ALLITERATION. Refers to the repetition of consonant sounds, particularly at the beginning of words, for example: "blistered and blackened," or "murmuring multitudes."

ANAPEST. A metrical foot consisting of two unstressed syllables followed by one stressed syllable, for example: "cig*arette*."

ASSONANCE. Refers to vowel sounds which are alike, as in the words "cold" and "lonely," or "vain" and "brave."

CONSONANCE. Patterns of consonants are alike, but vowel sounds are dissimilar, as in "rhymes" and "reams," or "trusting" and "trysting."

COUPLET. Two consecutive rhyming lines of poetry.

DACTYL. A metrical foot consisting of one accented syllable followed by two unaccented, for example: "*com*pensate."

DIMETER. A line of poetry consisting of two metrical feet.

END-STOPPED LINE. Refers to the end of a poetic line which coincides with a normal speech pause. Its opposite is a run-on line.

ENJAMBMENT. Another term for a run-on line.

EUPHONY. Pleasantness of sound.

FEMININE RHYME. Rhymed syllables are followed by unstressed final syllables that are identical, as in "curling" and "hurling," or "ocean" and "motion."

FOOT. See metrical foot.

HEPTAMETER. A line of poetry consisting of seven metrical feet.

HEXAMETER. A line of poetry consisting of six metrical feet.

IAMB. A metrical foot consisting of one unaccented syllable followed by one accented syllable, for example: "in*clude*."

INTERNAL RHYME. Rhyming that occurs within poetic lines rather than at the end.

MASCULINE RHYME. The rhyming occurs in the stressed final syllables of the words, as in "de*cide*" and "pre*side*."

METRE. Refers to the system of measuring rhythm in poetry, and in particular to the sound patterns of stressed and unstressed syllables.

METRICAL FOOT. The sound unit of metre. It always consists of one stressed syllable and one or more unstressed syllables. The four principal types of metrical feet are anapestic, dactylic, iambic, and trochaic.

MONOMETER. A line of poetry consisting of one metrical foot.

PENTAMETER. A line of poetry consisting of five metrical feet.

RUN-ON LINE. Occurs when the end of a poetic line does not coincide with a normal speech pause, but flows into the next line. Also called "Enjambment."

SLANT RHYME. An inexact or approximate rhyme, as in "wander" and "plunder," or "jive" and "give."

SONNET. A poem of fourteen lines, written in iambic pentameter.

SPONDEE. A metrical foot consisting of two accented syllables.

TETRAMETER. A line of poetry consisting of four metrical feet.

TRIMETER. A line of poetry consisting of three metrical feet.

TROCHEE. Describing a metrical foot in which one stressed syllable is followed by one unstressed syllable, for example: "*pur*pose."

INDEX TO POEMS